KATHLEEN
COOKE

P9-ELR-665

HOPE
4
TODAY

Stay Connected
to God in a
Distracted Culture

BroadStreet
PUBLISHING

BroadStreet Publishing® Group, LLC
Racine, Wisconsin, USA
BroadStreetPublishing.com

HOPE 4 TODAY: Stay Connected to God in a Distracted Culture

ISBN-13: 978-1-4245-5523-9 (faux leather)
ISBN-13: 978-1-4245-5524-6 (e-book)

Stock or custom editions of BroadStreet Publishing titles may be purchased in bulk for educational, business, ministry, fundraising, or sales promotional use. For information, please e-mail info@broadstreetpublishing.com.

Cover design by Chris Garborg at garborgdesign.com
Interior design and typesetting by Katherine Lloyd at theDESKonline.com

Printed in China

18 19 20 21 5 4 3 2 1

For my heavenly Father, my eternal love,

and Phil Cooke, my shelter and constant protector.

You're the love of my life.

You taught me to never settle.

FOREWORD

I have spent my entire adult life exploring research on those things an individual can do or a set of actions they can take in order for their behavior to radically change so that transformation happens. And no, I haven't been a Christ follower all those years. In fact, I hated Christians most of my professional life.

So imagine how surprised I was when I discovered after reviewing ten thousand surveys, including random samples of all ages of the general population in the US and then later around the world, that *how you handled your Bible was the best predictor of where you are spiritually.*

Now, after over one hundred thousand surveys, the fact remains that if you engage with your Bible (by reading, reflecting, and responding) four or more times a week, *scientifically* we know that your life looks radically different than everyone else's. In fact, the findings are so powerful it has changed everything we do here at Back to the Bible Ministries.

You may be saying to yourself, *So really, what Grandma said so many years ago, to read your Bible every day, really had scientific merit. Why?*

What we discovered is that those who engage the Bible four or more times a week consistently and over time biblically connect their heart to Jesus and their spiritual life starts kicking in at an entirely new level. I personally believe this is because the more time you spend engaging the Bible, the more opportunity you have to hear from the Holy Spirit.

The more you hear from the Holy Spirit in the context of

what God's Word says, the higher the likelihood you will get what He has to say right and your life starts to radically transform. And no, the Bible isn't the only way to hear from the Holy Spirit, but satan has the ability to appear as the angel of light and he is eliminated when you listen to the Holy Spirit in the context of God's Word.

People who claim to be Christians yet do not engage the Bible four or more times a week are far more likely to be following their own inclinations, meaning that oftentimes, they lead very troubled lives where Jesus makes very little sense at all. Better said: people who engage the Bible fewer than four times a week *appear* to have asked Jesus into their life, yet they go wherever their notions lead them.

By contrast, the four plus engagers pursue Jesus wherever He leads them the best way they know how, which is hearing from Him on a daily basis by connecting their heart to His words written just for them. And yes, eventually they get that peace that passes all understanding (Philippians 4:7) and do radical things like living the way Jesus instructs them to.

What I absolutely love about Kathleen Cooke is that she is doing everything she can to bring Jesus to the masses through media. Kathleen's efforts to help you to start biblically connecting your heart to Jesus is an awesome way of once again *bringing Jesus directly to the doorstep of your heart.*

Now, start engaging!

Dr. Arnie Cole
Chief Executive Officer, Back to the Bible Ministries
Lincoln, Nebraska

INTRODUCTION

*I*t was a Bible, but not just any Bible. The New Testament had belonged to Anne Boleyn (1501–1536), the second wife of King Henry VIII of England. The archivist gently placed it into my gloved hands and opened it. On a fragile page, the book's owner had written her name, *Anne*, in big gold letters that spanned from edge to edge. I wondered if she had done that in the darkness of the Tower of London before she was beheaded. Many had died before and many would die afterward for this precious book of books. A new reverence and awe for its words and promises sent a shiver up my spine.

I was in London filming *The Better Hour: The Legacy of William Wilberforce* (thebetterhour.org), a documentary for PBS, with our production company, Cooke Pictures. We were shooting historic documents of famous individuals and conducting interviews with historians, and it had been difficult getting to the British Library on that day, June 6, 2005. Security was at its highest. Bombs had exploded the day before in one of the worst terrorist attacks in London's history, with the Tube station where the bomb had killed and injured so many right nearby. Our appointment with the library had been the day before, and we were almost there when the bomb exploded. Had we not needed our film equipment and crew with us, which required that we rent a van that day, we would have been on that train.

I sat there holding Anne's Bible and thought about God's protection and providence. He had spared me the day before, and the biblical words of His protection came to mind: "Be strong and courageous. Do not be afraid or terrified because of them, for the LORD your God goes with you; he will never leave you nor forsake you" (Deuteronomy 31:6).

I wondered, *What Scripture was Anne thinking about when she died?*

God wrote the Bible for you. Do you value it?

This devotional is different from others that you may have read in the past. My hope is that you use it as a starting point to stimulate your thinking toward a deeper relationship with God, because we need courage and hope to live in our culture today more than ever. So why are there only four entries per week?

The Center for Bible Engagement (CBE) (backtothebible. org/research) conducted an eight-year study of more than one hundred thousand people to discover why so many people own Bibles yet so few read them. They also wanted to determine, from a scientific perspective, what difference it makes when people do or don't read Scripture. Their study polled individuals from eight to eighty years of age with comprehensive surveys that included questions about religious preference and beliefs, religious service attendance, engagement in prayer and Bible reading, daily temptations, and engagement in high-risk behaviors such as pornography and destructive thoughts.[1]

The best-selling book of all time, the Bible, is owned by 93 percent of Americans, with an average of four Bibles in each home.[2] Yet most never read it, especially outside of church. This is a critical problem because CBE research shows that engaging with the Bible four or more days a week is the strongest and most reliable way to grow spiritually.[3] Thus, our four devotionals per week.

Bible reading provides a level of protection against temptation and is correlated with less involvement in detrimental behaviors. If a person engages the Bible four or more times a week, their odds of giving in to temptation decreases, such as drinking to excess (62 percent less), viewing pornography (59 percent less), and having sex outside marriage (59 percent less).[4] As well, when people engage four or more times a week, it also produces more peace and joy in their life by reducing emotional struggles. Those who read God's Word regularly experience less fear and anxiety, struggle less with guilt, and are more forgiving of others.

So what does all this research really say to you and me? That if we engage in the Bible four times a week or more (personally read the Bible, one on one with God), we'll make significant positive choices and changes in our lives, more so than those who do not. The research also showed that when a person reads the Bible one to three times a week, it affects their life but not nearly as significantly. Listening to Christian music, watching religious programs, reading Christian books, and praying can certainly affect and contribute positively to life, but reading the Bible makes a statistical difference. This was particularly evident in teens (thirteen- to seventeen-year-olds) and tweens (eight- to twelve-year-olds).[5]

So why is it so hard to read the Bible, especially when we have access to it and so many in our homes? The number one reason is that we're too busy. This is followed closely by the second reason, that we're too distracted. We live in a media-driven, cluttered, and preoccupied world where we're bombarded with thousands of media messages a day.

We can't drive down the street, open a website, or go to the gas station, grocery store, or doctor's office without being subjected to advertisements. We simply can't escape them. Our technologies have also enabled us to do more, so we do. Our schedules are jam-packed with more than most of us can do each day. We stay up late trying to finish it all and then dash out of bed in the morning to finish what we didn't do the day before and won't be able to finish that day. Research shows that three-fourths of Christian young adults (ages eighteen to twenty-four) haven't read the entire Bible, and half of older adults (ages twenty-five and up) haven't either.[6] It's not a priority; it's not considered a matter of life or death.

But it is.

What if we thought of reading the Bible as a life-or-death matter? I wonder what the twenty-one martyred Egyptian Christian men who were beheaded by ISIS in May 2015[7] would say about that? And what would the many people in our world who have little or no access to the Bible, in countries where God's Word is banned and readers can open them only in secret places due to fear, have to say? What if we made reading the Bible the number one priority in our weekly lives? How would it change us—make our lives different?

As I thought about this, I was reminded of 2 Chronicles 12:14: "He did evil because he did not set his heart to seek the LORD." Is one of the reasons we're seeing such chaos erupting globally because we've failed to read God's Word and teach our children of its importance?

Some people may wonder why praying isn't enough to help us make right choices in life. The CBE research also concluded that prayer, even when combined with going to church, nurtures our relationship with Christ but doesn't lead to living in a Christlike way. Two-thirds (67.9 percent) of American adults pray at least once a day and two-fifths (40.1 percent) say they attend church at least once a month,[8] and while it's logical that these are important, they don't change behavior.

I desire a strong and healthy body, and I've even prayed about it. A gym membership followed, but I didn't see results until I actually exercised and ate the right healthy foods. I had to *engage* not just my heart but also my mind and will.

Christianity is not just about believing in God; it's also about having a relationship with God. And a relationship is what God desires most from us. A one-way conversation (us talking to God) is not a relationship. A relationship requires two-way conversation and spending time together. We can hear God's voice in prayer and in church, but by not reading the Bible, we limit ourselves. Bible reading solidifies and builds our spiritual muscle, and we must build it *at least four times a week* if we're to be strong and healthy spiritually.

The study also found that longtime Christ followers are sometimes hindered by not having someone who holds them accountable. Some didn't even know where to start in the Bible. Here's what one survey respondent said: "I think one of the main issues is that I don't always know the best way to go about reading the Bible and having it apply to/affect my life. This, along with time and energy. ... However, none of these are good, just excuses."[9]

Reading this, I again thought about my often-neglected exercise plans. I realized that when I shelled out my money for a gym membership, I went more often and was rewarded with a stronger, healthier body. I'm hoping that when you invest in this book, it, too, might be a starting point for you to engage in the Bible for yourself. We each need to decide if a system of rewards might assist with our spiritual health. Exercise trainers say that if people start with just a five-minute workout a day, it will change their health. Could you start with just five minutes with God four times a week? Think how it might change the direction of your life.

One of my kids' favorite children's books, *Five Minutes' Peace* by Jill Murphy, is about a mother elephant who wants five minutes to herself a day because the demands of her children and life are overwhelming. What if you took five minutes a day for

God's peace? Time is a precious possession because it affects everyone and everything. When will you take control of your time? Is it worth achieving a "peace ... which transcends all understanding" (Philippians 4:7)?

My prayer is that when you read this devotional, you don't see me, but will see God and know Him better. My hope is that you will become enthralled in reading His Word and knowing Him more deeply so that your hope in God will be strengthened. I challenge you to read not just the Scripture verse for every entry but the entire chapter, and allow God to take you on a unique journey with Him. Consider it not Bible-reading time but relationship-building time. Would you allow distractions to get in the way of time with your most cherished loved ones on earth? Of course not. So make God your most cherished relationship and see how your earthly cherished relationships become even stronger and more valuable. See how it changes everything as it brings clarity in new ways.

In my husband's book *One Big Thing: Discovering What You Were Born to Do*, he outlines how each of us has been created with a God-given purpose. Mine is to be a cheerleader, and I'm cheering you on as I share a bit about what I've learned from God on my life's journey. I'm sending up a heavenly shout that God's majesty and presence will envelop you as you determine to spend time in His Word four times a week (you choose which days). We put vacation dates, playdates, romantic dates, and every other kind of date on our calendars. Take out your mobile device or calendar of choice right now and schedule in four dates with God for this week. Maybe for next week too.

My schedule is always changing, and I need to stay flexible as I travel regularly, shooting media projects, meeting with clients, and speaking to groups globally. If I'm going to stick to anything, it needs to be on my calendar. In the production business, we send out to each participant involved in the film shoot a "call time"—the time they're to show up on set to work. By scheduling my Bible "call time" with God four times a week, it's not an afterthought but a "must show up on the set" time.

You may have a more consistent weekly schedule and might want your call time with God to have a routine day and time. For me, flexibility within my disruptive schedule allows me to be habitually consistent. Remember too that God doesn't want a relationship of bondage; He's a God of freedom.

Hope 4 Today: Stay Connected to God in a Distracted Culture will help you keep coming back to Him and His Word—the Wellspring of living water, the Bread of Life, and the Lamp to our feet. May our sweet Jesus lead you to His wisdom, a stronger relationship with Him, and a life that flourishes as a result of your obedience. God's grace and light go with you.

> May the God of hope fill you with
> all joy and peace as you trust in him,
> so that you may overflow with hope by
> the power of the Holy Spirit.
> ROMANS 15:13

WEEK

1

Day 1

ACTING OR BEING?

> Then he said to them all: "Whoever wants to be my disciple must
> deny themselves and take up their cross daily and follow me."
>
> LUKE 9:23

I watched from a window as the women scrubbed clothes in the muddy river. A cow waded upstream as children dodged trash on the bank. The smell of rotting garbage and sewage made it hard to breathe. New Life Church in Chennai, India, sits across the river, and I was climbing the stairs to the church offices when I stopped at an open window. I was teaching theatrical acting classes at a media conference sponsored by OneHope International,[10] and had been teaching students how to become the character instead of just acting the part. Having focused on taking in environments with all our senses, I took a deep choking breath and fixed my eyes on the river. I wanted to seal it all in my soul.

We often want to act the part as Christians. It's easy to observe from afar. But to be true followers of Christ, we need to get our hands dirty in the muddy, smelly water of life. As I stood there, my host explained that the church regularly has teams of people bring food, clothing, and medical supplies—along with the love of Jesus—to these people. While it is challenging work, many have been rescued and come to know Jesus.

■ ■ ■

Are you stopping at the window to take in the culture, or are you rushing past? What's one thing that you could do today to be the hands of God and not just act the part?

9

ADOPTED AND FREE

> For you did not receive the spirit of slavery to fall back into
> fear, but you have received the Spirit of adoption as sons, by
> whom we cry, "Abba! Father!"
>
> ROMANS 8:15 ESV

*W*hen I work with college internship students, I teach them about the need to have a servant spirit and do whatever is asked—to sit down, keep their mouths shut, and observe the culture of the office. The students pay attention to this advice so well that they can humble themselves too much and seem insecure and unambitious. Fear keeps them from asking questions and expressing what they'd like to learn. Employers tell me that it's not until the last workday of the internship that the students finally speak up. While the interns were adopted into the company, fear kept them enslaved and unable to fully take advantage of an opportunity to flourish.

God has adopted us as children of His kingdom. He wants us to ask Him questions and to be free to express ourselves to Him. Yes, we're committed to Him and want to serve Him fully, but He wants us to be knowledgeable, capable, and fearless—and yes, even argue with Him. He wants to mentor us, not make us robots.

■ ■ ■

Which of your deep desires are you holding back from your Father?
Break your servant chains and express yourself.

ADOPTING JEWELS

Do everything without grumbling or arguing,
so that you may become blameless and pure, "children of
God without fault in a warped and crooked generation."
Then you will shine among them like stars in the sky.

PHILIPPIANS 2:14–15

*T*ears spilled down her cheeks as she told me, "My mama gave me away. Why did she do that? Didn't she love me?" This little girl was a child of the foster care system and by the age of eight had lived in nine homes. But today she was being adopted by her forever family. She was not only being adopted by a committed Christian family but by the family's church. They, too, were dedicated to raising her to know Jesus. The local church was committed to helping the adoptive family because that's what Christians do; they're a united body.

The number of children in foster care in the United States is staggering. What if churches confronted the destruction of satan's evils and started winning this battle of rejection? What if they were the hands of God's redemption and grace on earth in a very powerful and real way? The government can't fix the problem because it's an issue of the heart, but Christians can. We know the Heart Surgeon, our Father who created our hearts and can mend them. He can also perform open heart surgery on us, allowing us to welcome a child into our lives. Is it painful and hard? You bet. Surgery is always painful, but the result is life.

◼ ◼ ◼

Do you have a spare bedroom? A spare place in your heart? Consider whether God is asking you to adopt a child or assist someone in raising up a child for God's kingdom.

AGAINST TYPE

I praise you because I am fearfully and wonderfully made;
your works are wonderful, I know that full well.

PSALM 139:14

I cast media projects for our production company in Hollywood. I am always looking for new and interesting personalities or types. *Typecasting* is the term Hollywood uses to describe an actor's natural look. Directors often cast roles solely because an actor looks like a cop, lawyer, or biker. But sometimes a TV show or movie requires casting against type. For example, Arnold Schwarzenegger plays an undercover kindergarten teacher in *Kindergarten Cop*, and Charlize Theron, a captivatingly beautiful woman, played a serial killer in her Academy Award-winning performance in *Monster*.

Have you ever thought that as Christians, we might turn people away because of how we present ourselves? God's blessed us all with uniqueness, but we may seem odd to others. Their fear of our type and sometimes even the language we use may create a wall and keep them from seeing the grace of Jesus. There are several Christian motorcycle gangs who at first glance seem abrasive, and I know a tough petite woman ministry worker who is caring for orphans amongst the bombs dropping in the Middle East. God uses all types to further His kingdom purposes, but He may ask us to play against our type so His kingdom can flourish. When we're authentic, it's easier for others to see Jesus in us.

■ ■ ■

How might you be keeping others from seeing God because of your lifestyle and looks? How might you be typecasting others and limiting God's purposes?

Journal

WEEK

2

Day 1

AN INKLING OF LOVE

And to know this love that surpasses knowledge—that you
may be filled to the measure of all the fullness of God.

EPHESIANS 3:19

*I*n the movie *Star Wars*, Han Solo had an inkling—a funny feeling about "the old man and the kid" (Obi-Wan Kenobi and Luke Skywalker). In the end, his knowledge of "the force" allowed him to find more than riches and fame; he also found purpose and love.

When God's force—the Holy Spirit—takes control of our lives, we find contentment, purpose, and ultimate love. In our chaotic world, God's ultimate plan is being fulfilled, but it requires three steps of faith.

First, we must recognize that He's the Supreme Authority; second, we need an unbreakable connection with Him; and third, we must act on the knowledge that God will complete His plan in us and not apart from Him.

God is not asking us to be spiritual; we're to be relational. He wants us to relate with our hearts, our minds, and our inklings of hope. Our heart knowledge synchronizes with our mind as we read His Word and spend time in prayer. Through the connection of prayer, we're able to take control of our lives to fight the forces that rage during chaotic circumstances. His force—the Holy Spirit—is with us.

■ ■ ■

Have you ever had an inkling of love that surpasses knowledge? Navigate in the knowledge of God's world, and may His Spirit be with you.

Day 2

ARMS OF FORGIVENESS

"So he got up and went to his father. But while he was still a long
way off, his father saw him and was filled with compassion for him;
he ran to his son, threw his arms around him and kissed him."

LUKE 15:20

"Standing in the middle of the runway with arms outstretched was my father," Heather Mercer told me over
coffee, describing the moment she was reunited with her dad
after being imprisoned in Afghanistan. She had been working
for a humanitarian agency when the Taliban arrested her and
threw her into a rat- and scorpion-infested prison. One of eight
hostages rescued in 2001, she had prayed for the day she'd see
her father again. God had placed the Afghan people on her
heart, and the threat of death didn't deter her, even though her
parents had strongly objected to her going there.

We make decisions every day, pushing known limits of wisdom and risk, and sometimes we make choices that seem to
others to be rebellious. Still, God uses our choices to shape
our future. The parable of the prodigal son (Luke 15:11–32)
has many lessons, but it's the father's open arms that always
stand out in the story. Heather's return to her father's arms was
sweet, but the arms of her heavenly Father held her throughout
her prison ordeal. His arms brought hope to her daily. And His
arms continue to shape her life today as she leads her own relief
agency, Hope for Iraq (hope4iraq.org).

■ ■ ■

*What life choices are you making today? Remember, the Father is
still with you and His arms are ever stretched out. Will you fall into
them?*

Day 3

AVOIDING TOE PAIN

Teach me to do your will, for you are my God;
may your good Spirit lead me on level ground.

PSALM 143:10

A few years ago, I was invited to a conference that was held at a ski lodge in Big Sky, Montana, in June. One afternoon several of us decided to ride the chair lift to the top of the mountain and then walk down (the snow had mostly melted). I thought it would be easy, until my toes began to ache inside my soaking-wet shoes. The constant pressure of pushing down on the tips of my toes to maintain balance was excruciating. I was never so happy to be back on level ground.

Most of us know that walking uphill is difficult, but walking straight down can be equally painful. The same is true with our spiritual life. We know the pain of climbing to the top of the mountain to God, so we avoid it. But we put ourselves in greater pain by walking away—downhill from Him. Trusting God and His will requires spiritual balance. Our lazy souls like to stay on level ground, but God requires that we keep moving up and be spiritually fit to climb life's mountains with Him. God is at the top, and He wants us up there with Him. And once we're there? The view's awesome!

■ ■ ■

Are you climbing up or walking down today? What do you need to do each day to keep heading uphill (or to get yourself turned around)?

17

INTERPRETERS FOR JESUS

Then Jesus declared, "… I have come down from heaven not
to do my will but to do the will of him who sent me."

JOHN 6:35, 38

*A*ccording to research, approximately 6,909 distinct languages exist in the world today.[11] Interestingly, missionaries have done much of the work in finding and documenting these languages so the Bible can be translated.

There are also cultural languages spoken by people as close as next door. But we never engage with them because their language is so foreign. Urban slang is so common now that one online dictionary, which started as a joke, is now used in courts to interpret court cases.[12] Christians have their own language as well. Words like *fellowship*, *justification*, and *sanctification* often aren't understandable to the unchurched.

God is asking us to take the time to learn how to speak to those around us and be interpreters of His truth. That's what Jesus did; He came to earth as an interpreter. He put on human skin so He could speak our language. And if God could do that for us, isn't it time we break down the cultural language barriers around us so we can reach others for Him?

■ ■ ■

How can you start learning the language of the culture? Consider ways to learn the cultural language and build relationships with those around you so you can bring the awesome sauce of Jesus to them.

Journal

WEEK

3

AWESOMENESS OF GOD

> However, as it is written: "What no eye has seen, what no
> ear has heard, and what no human mind has conceived"—
> the things God has prepared for those who love him.
>
> 1 CORINTHIANS 2:9

*A*wesome! This word is used so often today that its powerful meaning has diminished. Now everything is awesome— my haircut, my kids' finger painting, and my BBQ sandwich. Long ago there were people who actually saw the awesomeness of God; they physically saw Him.

Coptic Christians can be traced to the beginnings of Christianity. Some believe as far back as the magi at the birth of Christ. Their artwork has encouraged the faith of many and can be found in many Egyptian churches today. It is characteristically known by its depiction of people with enlarged eyes, ears, and heads, signifying their spiritual relationship with God. Coptic eyes are painted particularly big to reflect the awe of God—His wonder, majesty, and awesomeness.

The next time you hear something described as *awesome*, stop and think about the mind-blowing true awesomeness of God. Do you love Him? Trust Him? God's preparing something special for you that you could *never* conceive. Now *that* is an awesome thought!

■ ■ ■

How can you keep your eyes open fully on God? What might you do to show someone this week just how awesome He truly is?

Day 2

BABBLING PRAYERS

"And when you pray, do not keep on babbling like pagans, for
they think they will be heard because of their many words."

MATTHEW 6:7

*F*or many years I attended The Church On The Way in Los
Angeles when Jack Hayford (Pastor Jack) was lead pastor.
He started prayer circles during services, where groups of four
to five participants would be given approximately ten minutes
to pray together. Every once in a while, someone would take the
entire time going on and on about their needs, or they'd think
they were particularly holy and needed to prove their spiritu-
ality to the circle. Then there were people who said, "Father
God," "Holy Father," or "dear Jesus" after every other word. The
prayer circles were always interesting, and they taught me how
to pray in a group.

Matthew 6:7 tells us that God wants to hear from our hearts
when we pray. Our words should be spontaneous and authentic, especially when we pray in a group. One of the reasons we
struggle with praying in groups is because we don't pray enough
in private; we haven't learned how to have a real conversation
with God. When we have an intimate connection, we should
pray as freely as we speak to our parents, children, and close
friends. We don't have to repeat His name after every short
phrase or sound lofty to gain attention. A comfortable relationship with God testifies of a trusted and confident knowledge of
God's presence.

■ ■ ■

*How much time do you spend in prayer each day? Pray more, and
do it out loud. Build your relationship with God and have a real
conversation.*

Day 3

BE A GODLY MENTOR

Whoever refreshes others will be refreshed.

PROVERBS 11:25

*O*ne summer at a family reunion in the mountains, my younger daughter, at age fourteen, sat on a boat dock surrounded by her cousins. They were captivated as she told them the secrets of being a teen; she was older and wiser, and they all wanted to be like her.

I have a college degree in education, and in recent years, while teaching college students, I've learned the truth of the phrase "You never really learn something until you teach it to someone else." Each time I teach something to students, I am reminded again of its importance and it's reinforced again in me, making me a better leader and mentor.

You're never too old or too young to mentor someone. Often, as we get older and busy with our lives, we forget that no matter what our past has been like, we've learned a thing or two and we can have an influence on others. God has taught us lessons and blessed us with skills and talents that can influence someone's life. And He promises that when we do, it will refresh us—inspire us even more.

If you feel stuck, mentor someone.

■ ■ ■

Where could you reach out and mentor someone? What's one thing that God has taught you that you can share to inspire someone else?

Day 4

GOD'S POWER SOURCE

"I am the LORD, and there is no other;
apart from me there is no God. I will strengthen you."

ISAIAH 45:5

*C*reative ideas, new approaches, and lofty visions drive culture. We are attracted to visionaries. In media and entertainment, creativity rules. Technology might be thought of as the flesh, and creativity as the blood of a project. While I may think I know how to shoot a film project with the latest camera, or write dialogue for a script on a computer, if I lack creativity, I will ultimately fail. The best of technology won't inspire and connect with audiences by itself.

In many ways, I view my physical being—my body that God created—to be His organic technology. He designed my soul to have His creative blood flowing through me to accomplish His purposes, and it's His creative blood that allows me to be a success artistically. If I'm not plugged into God's energy source, I'm disconnected and unable to creatively function. That's why I'd encourage you to stay connected to Him through prayer and reading His Word. Creative energy and strength flows when we're plugged into God's power source.

■ ■ ■

How often do you connect to God's power source? How does it affect your artistic talent and work if you're unplugged? Recharge yourself today by reading Isaiah chapter 45.

Journal

WEEK

4

Day 1

BOLT THE DOOR

At daybreak, Jesus went out to a solitary place. The people
were looking for him and when they came to where he was,
they tried to keep him from leaving them.

LUKE 4:42

I've been honored to meet great women of God in the
media business over the years. One of them is Lady Tracie
Edmiston, who founded Christian Vision (cvglobal.co), with
her husband, Lord Robert Edmiston. They work tirelessly for
the kingdom of God.

When I asked Tracie how she manages everything, she said, "I
have to bolt the door. Bob and I have to lock ourselves away and
shut out the noise and demands that at times are difficult to ignore.
Time with God has to be our priority. It's the only way we can continue to do what He's called us to do and not what we want to do."

Jesus also escaped crowds of people to spend time with the
Father. The deafening needs of the people that followed Him
must have been overwhelming. And though He had the ability to
fix their problems instantly, He knew His mission wasn't to do
what He wanted; He was under the instructions of His Father.

For many of us, giving comes naturally. Restraining ourselves can be difficult, but God may be asking us to do that to
complete His ultimate plan. Bolting the door and following His
will may be required so we can know and follow His will and
not our own.

■ ■ ■

*How do you react to the relentless needs where God's placed you? Bolt
the door and see what His perfect will is, then meet the needs.*

Day 2

BREAKING AND EMPTYING

A woman came with an alabaster jar of very expensive
perfume, made of pure nard. She broke the jar and poured
the perfume on his head.

MARK 14:3

Mary came with an alabaster jar and not only poured its contents out all over Jesus' head, she also shattered it. She spared none of the precious oil or the costly jar, for God spared nothing to bring our redemption. She was confident that Jesus would conquer death. The oil wouldn't be needed any longer to prepare dead bodies. He'd come to bring life—and life eternal.

How did Mary know? She was observant. She was listening. She was discerning. She had seen His miracles, heard His words, and understood His stories and teachings. When His beloved disciples were still missing His cues, she didn't. What kind of nonverbal communication did she and Jesus have that night that wasn't recorded—the unspoken words of her heart and the heart of God?

Mary shattered her soul and emptied herself at Jesus' feet so He could fill her soul with His complete love and presence. Today it's the fragrance of Jesus that permeates our air. Jesus wants us to come by breaking and emptying ourselves to Him. When we're completely shattered of ourselves, empty and given to Him, then new life begins. It's miraculous.

■ ■ ■

*Can you shatter your soul at His feet and let Him fill your vessel?
Empty yourself and see new life emerge.*

Day 3

LISTEN TO THE SILENCE

Wait for the Lord;
be strong and take heart and wait for the Lord.

PSALM 27:14

*S*ilent retreats are becoming popular. These are weekend (or sometimes longer) destination retreats where you don't talk to anyone, listen to the radio, watch TV, or use media devices. Our lives are filled with constant noise, media clutter, and distractions, and these retreats provide a way to disconnect.

We crave silence and yet we're scared to death of it. After all, what might we be forced to think about that our noisy lives allow us to otherwise avoid? We know the constant clutter of media isn't healthy to our mental, emotional, and spiritual lives, but actually following through and truly kicking it to the curb for a few days is terrifying.

Even so, I encourage you to do it. God is in the silence. The lack of noise will change and grow your spiritual awareness in new ways as you fine-tune your ears to the Holy Spirit. Try adding a food fast with it. God has some things He'd like to talk to you about if you could just stop, breathe, and disconnect. Listen to the silence.

■ ■ ■

Silence is golden. How can you add more silence to your life so you can listen and feel the Spirit of God anew in your being?

STORY WATER

When a Samaritan woman came to draw water,
Jesus said to her, "Will you give me a drink?"
JOHN 4:7

*J*esus told stories to give us a glimpse of His Father. His intent was to teach those who would be on the earth after He was gone how to receive His redemptive life and know His Father's love. His example and teachings still live on because they were written down.

One of my favorite Bible stories is the woman at the well. Jesus waits until the heat of the day to chat with her. He knew her story, that of a woman failing and broken. She wasn't a village elder but had significant influence with a specific group of people that He wanted to reach. She was a leader with the outcasts. Those who had lost hope and needed fresh living water and to write a new chapter in their storybook.

We need to write our stories down too. Every day we live, we write a new page in our storybook—we add water into the well that God can use to bring His truths to others. God is asking you to leave His legacy to be read by those yet to come. He wants us to leave a well others can dip into to grasp the truths of Jesus.

■ ■ ■

What words of life would you write for others to read of how God's proven Himself? Dip your pen into the well of His living water and write down your faith story.

Journal

WEEK

5

Day 1

BUT ... IT DOESN'T MAKE SENSE!

And the peace of God, which transcends all understanding,
will guard your hearts and your minds in Christ Jesus.

<small>PHILIPPIANS 4:7</small>

My mom was raised in the traditions of the Catholic church, but it wasn't until my brother was born and my parents moved to Las Vegas that my mom formed a vibrant personal relationship with God. She'd grown up knowing about her Maker, but now she was in constant communication with Him. Having a sick child (my brother was born without a heart valve, and his longevity was uncertain) and living in a dry desert town on a teacher's salary kept her on her knees. Prayer kept her grounded, and God's Word brought unnatural confidence. She had a peace that could only come from trust in God, and her unshakable faith was an example to me and those she met.

Life will have unfathomable challenges. That's a given. But God never moves. He's with us in the deserts, the disasters, and the uncertainties. And He'll continue to be there to take us through every situation. His peace is only a breath away. While my brother died in just a few short years, Mom's faith never did. God's promise of eternal life kept her confident that "neither death nor life ... will be able to separate us from the love of God" (Romans 8:38–39). That same faith and confidence can be yours as well.

■ ■ ■

What in your life doesn't make sense to you? How can you trust God to transcend your uncertainty? Give Him control of your heart and mind—trust Him.

BE CAREFUL WHAT YOU SEE

> "I tell you that anyone who looks at a woman lustfully has
> already committed adultery with her in his heart."
>
> MATTHEW 5:28

When I was eight years old, I found my older brother's *Playboy* magazines hidden under his bed. Sadly, eight is also the average age that children are exposed to pornography today.[13] I was raised in a family that went to church every week, and in Sunday school, we sang: "Oh, be careful little eyes what you see." I couldn't unsee what was in those magazines, and children today are no different. That experience affected me, and it affects greater numbers of children today.

The billion-dollar pornography business is out of control globally. The explosive growth of the industry over the years is truly frightening, and pornography today is raw, violent, and sadistic. And once exposure begins, the claws of addiction quickly grow and the need for more perverted stimulation intensifies.

God knows that what we see affects our heart and in turn our minds, and His direct warnings reflects His love for us. He desires that we keep our lives pure and good so our actions toward others will be pure and good. First Corinthian 6:18 warns us to "flee from sexual immorality." In Matthew 6:22 Jesus tells us that "the eye is the lamp of the body." And Proverbs 4:23 says, "Guard your heart, for everything you do flows from it."

■ ■ ■

Jesus healed the eyes of the blind, and He continues to heal eyes today. What things have you seen that have affected you? Flee to Him for healing.

Day 3

CAUSE AND EFFECT

Command those who are rich in this present world
not to be arrogant nor to put their hope in their wealth,
which is so uncertain, but to put their hope in God,
who richly provides us with everything for our enjoyment.
Command them to do good, to be rich in good deeds,
and to be generous and willing to share.

1 TIMOTHY 6:17–18

*C*ause and effect. This law of physics is well known, and it can be applied not just to our physical life but also to our spiritual one. What determines a positive effect over a negative one is often our will.

Looking back over my life, I see strategic choices and how they affected the outcomes. When I chose my way and a momentary selfish desire, I found discontent. But each time I chose to forego what the world would view as happiness and chose to walk in God's will, life flourished with abundant joy. Happiness is temporary, but joy is eternal. Time and again when God closes down what seems to make us happy, He does so to bring something better.

God asks us to choose to trust His highest good, to choose to trust His way (which isn't always the easy way), and to be mindful that when success comes, we are to give. Share His abundance generously and put His will first. When we choose the cause for Christ, the effect is untold joy.

■ ■ ■

What has caused you to abandon hope? Was it because you chose temporary happiness over eternal joy? Choosing lasting joy often starts with self-denial and a generous spirit.

Day 4

CEASE THE BLAME GAME

When tempted, no one should say, "God is tempting me."
For God cannot be tempted by evil, nor does he tempt
anyone; but each person is tempted when they are dragged
away by their own evil desire and enticed.

JAMES 1:13–14

*G*od must hate me! Why did God do this? Have these thoughts ever crossed your mind? If so, remember that humans often blame God for things He didn't cause. We live in a "pass the blame" culture, and no one is exempt—even God. But the truth is we live in a fallen, sinful world and we often choose not to resist sin.

King David understood that we all have a sinful nature and willingly accepted his punishment. In 2 Samuel 24:24 he confessed that he was responsible and must pay the cost of his sin: "I will not sacrifice to the LORD my God burnt offerings that cost me nothing." He wouldn't blame God for His sin, knowing he made the choice and so he had to pay for them.

James 4:7 says, "Submit yourselves, then, to God. Resist the devil, and he will flee from you." Know that Jesus will return one day to defeat the devil and restore the earth. Until then, we will fail and must bathe in God's grace and mercy. Jesus came to earth to teach us how to navigate this messy world, so devour His Word and pray ceaselessly. Cease the blame game, and remember that His forgiveness and mercy are everlasting, but sometimes you must suffer the consequences of your choices.

■ ■ ■

What have you blamed God or someone else for in your life? Get over it by confessing it, being willing to pay for your mistakes, and then watch God transform the situation.

Journal

WEEK

6

CHAMPIONS OF FAITH

David said to the Philistine, "You come against me with
sword and spear and javelin, but I come against you
in the name of the LORD Almighty, the God of the armies
of Israel, whom you have defied."

1 SAMUEL 17:45

Dietrich Bonhoeffer was a Lutheran pastor, theologian, and poet who was martyred for the cause of Christ in a Nazi prison camp during World War II, just two weeks shy of being liberated. His writings continue to inspire and teach us how to live boldly as Christians today. One of my favorite quotes of his is "He who believes does not flee," which he based on Isaiah 28:16.[14]

The Bible is full of stories of champions of our faith who courageously stepped into life-threatening situations. I think of Stephen, Paul, and our Savior, Jesus Christ. While most of us today are not fleeing from eminent death because we've shared the truth of Jesus with someone, many people are in other parts of the world.

Do you unquestionably believe in the Lord? Christians are being martyred globally as never before for their faith in God. In your busy schedule today, be mindful of and pray for those who are boldly giving their lives for the cause of Christ. Stand with our champions of the faith and become one yourself.

■ ■ ■

What would you do if someone put a gun to your head and asked if you believed in Jesus Christ? Would you deny Him? Affirm your beliefs to be a champion of faith.

Day 2

STUBBORN CHANGES

Not that I have already obtained all this, or have already
arrived at my goal, but I press on to take hold of that
for which Christ Jesus took hold of me.

PHILIPPIANS 3:12

*C*hange is hard.

Dr. Koon Teo, chief cardiologist at McMaster University
Medical Centre in Hamilton, Ontario, has published exten-
sive research proving this in the *Journal of the American Medical
Association*. After five years, only 4.3 percent of heart attack
patients will be exercising, following a healthy diet, and not
smoking.[15] Within five years, people are back at it. Even the
threat of death doesn't make most people change their lifestyle.

The issues and barriers that keep us from real change can
include fear, insecurity, past failures, family history, lack of education, genetics, and an unending myriad of other habits and
causes. For real change to happen, we need more than wishes
and resolutions; we have to embrace a higher power. God is our
only hope. Real transformation often requires a healing of our
soul, and that can only be done through God's intervention.

So grab God's passionate desire for you to be whole and living a flourishing life, then press on daily and speak His scriptural
promises. They're His infusions of real change. Never forget that
God is right at your side, and His grace is everlasting.

■ ■ ■

*What things do you want to change in your life? Ask God to show you
what Scriptures to memorize so you can reach His goals for your life.*

Day 3

A CHEATIN' HEART

Similarly, anyone who competes as an athlete
does not receive the victor's crown except
by competing according to the rules.

2 TIMOTHY 2:5

*C*ountry music singer/songwriter Hank Williams wrote the 1952 hit song *Your Cheatin' Heart*, but racing cyclist Lance Armstrong succumbed to one. He won the excruciating Tour de France seven consecutive times, from 1999 to 2005, but was banned for life and stripped of his wins after he was found to have cheated. In recent years, the race has continued to be plagued with cheaters. Some dishonest cyclists have even used tiny hidden motors to assist them in climbing steep hills.[16]

There's a crown Christians are competing for, and not one on this earth: "the crown of glory that will never fade away" (1 Peter 5:4). We're born into this world competing from our first breath of life, and we instinctually compete for everything.

The one thing we'll never have to compete for is the love and forgiveness of God. He "shows no partiality to princes and does not favor the rich over the poor, for they are all the work of his hands" (Job 34:19). God's heart is big enough for all of us—even the cheatin' ones.

■ ■ ■

How have you been a cheater? Come clean by asking for God's grace and mercy today.

Day 4

CHEERS FROM HEAVEN

What, then, shall we say in response to these things?
If God is for us, who can be against us?

ROMANS 8:31

*W*ant to lose weight? Get a better job? Go back to college? Find a spouse? Get closer to God? Goals are great, but we live in a culture that wants instantaneous results. Often, if reaching a goal seems too daunting, we give up.

Whatever the challenge, real change is one of the most difficult battles you can fight. Before you start your journey, ask yourself specifically what you want to accomplish and how God can help you make those changes if it's His will.

Fans and cheerleaders bring inspiration to those sweating it out in the game, and often their encouragement can change the game's outcome. God's cheering for you each step of the way and wants you to be successful. He wants to make those difficult choices easy for you, but don't go it alone. Let Him be your loudest fan and cheerleader.

Then keep an eye out for His rewards—those little things He brings about along the way to encourage you. See the big goal as a series of mini goals, and celebrate them with God, who makes all things possible (Matthew 19:26).

■ ■ ■

What mini battle can God help you conquer today? Know that He's cheering you on from heaven.

Journal

WEEK

7

REJOICE!

Rejoice always.
1 THESSALONIANS 5:16

For four summers, I was honored to travel with a group of media professionals to multiple cities in India to teach acting classes to Christians wanting to learn how to use media more effectively. One of our hosts was a precious woman who worked as a women's leader at the church where the event took place each year. She wore a never-ending smile, and her compassionate heart throbbed with the love of Jesus. I'll never forget the beautiful prayers she'd pray at our team's meals.

Life for her and her family was challenging, but she had infectious joy. She didn't expect life to be easy or without suffering, loneliness, and uncertainty. Obtaining happiness from worldly possessions wasn't an option for her, so she sought God's joy. She had barely enough to survive each day, so she focused on the One who never disappoints—her heavenly Father. She knew that her joy could only be found in her relationship with God, and that He was the only true security in her uncertain world.

God is faithful and trustworthy even as our world today seems to be crumbling. He's our ever-present Hope in times of disasters, famine, poverty, and war. Rejoice always!

■ ■ ■

What are you wanting from life today? Are you mistaking and choosing momentary happiness for everlasting joy? Choose God's kingdom first.

Day 2

CHOOSE YOUR ENDING

This means that anyone who belongs to Christ has become
a new person. The old life is gone; a new life has begun.

2 CORINTHIANS 5:17 NLT

*H*ollywood studios spend millions of dollars each year
shooting multiple endings to films. They then set up
test screenings, and if audiences decide they don't like how the
movie ends, they just pop in a new version.

The choices I've made in my life haven't always been the
best ones, and sometimes I wish I could edit out the bad ones
and pop in new versions. Unfortunately, in real life we have to
live with our choices.

I recently met an ex-porn star who became a follower of
Jesus. She walked away from her previous lifestyle, but her past
choices continue to haunt her on the Internet. It's tough for her
to live in her redeemed godly life, and she has to continuously
hold fast to the Bible's promises that she's been forgiven and
restored even though the scars remain.

It takes guts to make godly choices. We get so imbedded in
life's darkness that finding the light to get out can be so scary
that we don't even try. We need to keep our eyes on Jesus and
trust His new ending—the perfect conclusion to our story.
Hollywood doesn't always get the ending right even after several tries, but God does. Always.

■ ■ ■

*What's one choice you could change today that would bring a new
ending in your life?*

46

JUSTICE FOR ALL

I urge, then, first of all, that petitions, prayers, intercession
and thanksgiving be made for all people—for kings and
all those in authority, that we may live peaceful and
quiet lives in all godliness and holiness.

1 TIMOTHY 2:1–2

*L*iving in this world, we're subject to government rule, and under kings, presidents, or rulers, that will never be ideal. God's perfect kingdom will come eventually, but until then we must endure. Paul sent a letter to Timothy, encouraging him to teach the early Christians to prepare and how they should respond to injustice.

First, we're to pray, for both the good rulers and the evil leaders. Second, we're to give thanks for them. Ouch! Can we really thank God for the harmful ones? Martin Luther King Jr. and Nelson Mandela are two men who demonstrated how to pray when injustice is inflicted. They were led by Scripture and by the example of Jesus, who was unjustly convicted and died that we might have eternal justice. The beheading of twenty-one Egyptian Christian pastors in Libya by ISIS in 2015 will be long remembered. They refused to deny Christ and died singing praises to Jesus. The Bible tells us that injustice will increase, but it's the testimony of God's ultimate victory that will never be forgotten. God's keeping score so we don't have to. His justice will prevail, so let Him be the final Judge.

■ ■ ■

What leaders do you need to be praying for? Pray with thanksgiving for all in authority. It brings hope and baffles the world.

Day 4

CLIMB MOUNTAINS

How beautiful on the mountains are the feet
of those who bring good news, who proclaim peace,
who bring good tidings, who proclaim salvation,
who say to Zion, "Your God reigns!"

<small>ISAIAH 52:7</small>

I love to climb the canyons near my home. While it's tough-going some mornings, I look forward to the view when I reach the top. For humans, there's something instinctual about wanting to climb high. We're an ambitious race, always pushing ourselves to new heights on the corporate ladder and physically.

Moses went up the mountain to speak to God as he led the children of Israel through the desert, and Jesus would take off for the hills to seek His Father. Our Creator designed us to look up as we climb, and to bring the good news of Jesus to others as we do. Our feet are called beautiful when we bring His peace and hope and the promise of Zion and God's salvation.

Psalm 40:2 says, "He lifted me out of the slimy pit, out of the mud and mire; he set my feet on a rock and gave me a firm place to stand." Follow Him to the top of the mountain. He's placed your feet on firm ground, and He's waiting to have a chat with you.

■ ■ ■

Write down ten things God has done for you that you can proclaim from your mountaintop. Thank Him, and share these with others.

Journal

WEEK

8

CLOUD WATCHING

Why, you do not even know what will happen tomorrow.
What is your life? You are a mist that appears
for a little while and then vanishes.

JAMES 4:14

*W*hen I was a kid, seatbelt laws were nonexistent. On trips, I'd lie in the back of my parents' station wagon and watch the cloud formations, trying to make faces out of them. Sometimes the clouds moved slowly and other times quickly, but they never looked the same. Then when I lived in Oklahoma as a college student, I experienced tornados and gained a greater respect for clouds and the weather that can come from them.

Clouds are much like our lives on earth, as James pointed out. They're mists. God is often associated with clouds in the Bible. Nahum 1:3 says, "The LORD is slow to anger but great in power; the LORD will not leave the guilty unpunished. His way is in the whirlwind and the storm, and clouds are the dust of his feet." His ways are mysterious and changing and yet His power is consistent, just like the clouds. This is why we need to consistently be in touch with Him. We must read His Word and be watchful. We are but a mist here for a short while.

■ ■ ■

When you're gone, will your life leave a storm or a covering of peaceful shade? How can you make sure your life isn't just floating by like the clouds?

COAL IN YOUR STOCKING

You, Lord, are forgiving and good,
abounding in love to all who call to you.

PSALM 86:5

As a child, I was told that Santa would put coal in my stocking if I wasn't good. But as hard as I tried, I knew I wasn't as good as I should be. Fortunately, I also knew Santa loved me and was forgiving.

God doesn't bring us coal, but He also doesn't always give us what we want. God brings us what He wills, and it's that truth that we wrestle with in life, especially when something devastating happens. Why doesn't He fix it, make it go away, heal it, bring that miracle? Why wouldn't it be His will?

How can we know the mind of God? We can't, and we won't. We just have to trust Him and learn how to think like He does. To do that, we need to have a vibrant relationship with Him. I've been a believer for over fifty years, and I'm still getting to know how He thinks. He never stops surprising me. Our joy is that He formed us and He knows what's best for us. As the psalmist said, "the LORD God is a sun and a shield; the LORD bestows favor and honor; no good thing does he withhold from those whose walk is blameless" (Psalm 84:11). In other words, He's our Protector even when we've made mistakes. He blesses us with gifts that are everlasting and just what we need

■ ■ ■

Has "coal" ended up in the stocking of your life? Burn that coal to light the fire of God in your life and see God's gifts more clearly.

Day 3

SURRENDER

Being confident of this, that he who began
a good work in you will carry it on to completion
until the day of Christ Jesus.

PHILIPPIANS 1:6

*S*urrender Dorothy. This was the message the Wicked Witch
of the West wrote in the sky with her broomstick as
Dorothy, the Scarecrow, the Tin Man, and the Cowardly Lion
journeyed to the Emerald City in the classic 1939 film *The
Wizard of Oz*. The special effect was achieved by using a hypo-
dermic needle to spread black ink across the bottom of a glass
tank filled with tinted water.[17]

Think about your own life. Have you surrendered, or are
you holding back because you're afraid God will end the fun
or take away your stuff (stuff that you think gives you security,
influence, and power)? Maybe you're dependent on that stuff,
even though you know you should be completely dependent on
Him for your value.

Give it up, "Dorothy." Surrender and trust the King of restoration and contentment. He's called you to walk *with* Him, not
on your own or in front of Him with your stuff. God has everlasting treasures for you, but you have to follow Him to attain His
eternal stuff. Your name is not written in some colored water that
will disperse or even in the sky where it will drift away; it's written in the eternal Book of Life. Your forever home is in heaven.
Remember what Dorothy learned: "There's no place like home."

■ ■ ■

What are you afraid to let go of, and why? Surrender and trust God.

Day 4

COMPELLED

"Now that I, your Lord and Teacher, have washed your feet,
you also should wash one another's feet."

<small>JOHN 13:14</small>

*C*hristianity is the only religious faith on the planet that doesn't require you to do anything but confess your sin and accept Jesus Christ as the redeemer and only Son of God. Acts 16:31 says, "Believe in the Lord Jesus, and you will be saved." There are no other must-dos.

But if you're a true believer and want a relationship with God, I believe you will be compelled to do five things:

1. Read your Bible regularly—at least four times a week. When you love someone, you want to spent time with them and know them intimately.

2. Pray often. There's no technique, formula, or set daily amount. Jesus gave an example—the Lord's Prayer—but He loves it when you speak and worship Him with all your heart.

3. Fast occasionally. Fasting is about your relationship with God and drawing closer to Him, and it doesn't always involve abstaining from food.

4. Give. It's not about money; it's about where your treasure is and the attitude you have when you give.

5. Share. If you're passionate about something, you tell others.

Jesus taught us to do all these things, then humbled Himself to the lowest of servants by washing His disciples' feet.

■ ■ ■

How can you build a relationship with God by serving Him?

Journal

WEEK

9

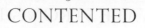

Day 1

CONTENTED

I am not saying this because I am in need, for I have learned
to be contented whatever the circumstances.

PHILIPPIANS 4:11

I don't want to get out of bed. The world's going crazy, and I can't ever get ahead. I want to escape. Escaping reality is one of the top things we fantasize about as adults. It's why tech companies are racing to create the best augmented-reality glasses—to allow people to escape.

Paul, on the other hand, wanted no part of this. He went for the grit and the suffering, propelled by his passion. He experienced difficult living conditions, walked thousands of miles, rode donkeys and camels, and sat in leaking boats, only to be thrown into prison and later executed. Even so, he learned to be contented.

He could have reworded the above verse this way: "I've been educated by my experience to be contained with God's provisions." Paul educated himself to be contented by containing his heart and mind on God's perfect will for him. If your heart is filled with Jesus, He'll be your contentment. But if you fill your heart and mind with what you (or culture) thinks you need, you'll be constantly striving and living a stressed-out, discontented life.

Stop trying to do things *for God*; He wants to do things *for you*—His timing and His way. When you begin to understand this, you'll lose interest in the stuff that culture dictates you must have for happiness. You'll stop living in momentary happiness and begin living in eternal contentment. Paul found his inside a prison cell. You can find it too.

■ ■ ■

What are some things of joy that God has given you? Seek godly desires, and watch your heart and mind be contained. Escape to contentment.

Day 2

CULTIVATE STRONG HANDS

"Just as you, Judah and Israel, have been a curse among
the nations, so I will save you, and you will be a blessing.
Do not be afraid, but let your hands be strong."

ZECHARIAH 8:13

ield of Dreams, the 1989 fantasy baseball film, was about
restoring hope for an Iowa farmer. "If you build it, they
will come," were the haunting words Ray (Kevin Costner) heard
in his vision of building a baseball diamond in the middle of a
cornfield.[18]

Zechariah also had a vision. His messages about the restoration of the temple are relevant today—both the physical
brick-and-mortar- temple and Jesus Christ, the living Temple.
Zechariah was influential in championing the people of his time
to not just restore Solomon's temple but also to restore their
identity of who they were in God. The world they lived in had
no language for God and didn't see God's purposes because of
the people's preoccupation with themselves. We live in a similar
culture today, a post-Christian era that has no understanding of
who Jesus is or of God's plan to restore humankind.

Zechariah's prophetic message stirred the people's imagi-
nations and brought assurance and a fresh reminder that God
has an eternal plan. These messages turned the people's hearts
toward the *magnificent* God of clarity, eternal restoration, and
peace. He made them rethink hope—to have strong hands.

■ ■ ■

*Zechariah's name means "God remembers." What is God helping you
remember that can bring you hope today as you face uncertain times?*

CULTURAL TRANSLATOR

> "God did this so that they would seek him and perhaps reach
> out for him and find him, though he is not far from any one of
> us. 'For in him we live and move and have our being.' As some
> of your own poets have said, 'We are his offspring.'"

*P*aul was a cultural translator. He recognized that to reach
the culture of his time, he'd need to use their language,
sometimes that of the poets. Paul didn't immerse himself in
their practices or beliefs, but he understood what was trending
and what consumed the people's time. In order for the Greeks
to understand who Jesus was, Paul had to use not just their verbal language but their cultural language.

Are you speaking the language of your culture? Often those
of us who have been raised in Christianity and its cultural influences don't recognize to what extent our worldview is different. We can live side by side and never speak to one another
because of a language barrier. Expressions like "a mighty time
of fellowship" and "washed in the blood of the Lamb" can be
confusing and even scary to nonbelievers.

Paul used stories that the culture would understand, and we
need to do the same. All have sinned and need the forgiveness
of God; people just have to be told this in a language they know.

■ ■ ■

How well do you understand the language of the culture you live in?
Study and observe how people communicate, then tell them about
Jesus in their language. Become a cultural translator of God's redemp-
tive story.

Day 4

CYBER SHAMING

Jesus straightened up and asked her,
"Woman, where are they?
Has no one condemned you?" "No one, sir," she said.
"Then neither do I condemn you," Jesus declared.
"Go now and leave your life of sin."

JOHN 8:10–11

Monica Lewinsky made history in 1998 when she had an affair with her boss, Bill Clinton, former president of the United States. But she was totally ill-prepared for what would occur next—the birth of cyberbullying. It was, as she calls it, her "ground zero moment."[19] Never before had the Internet usurped traditional media sources for information, heaping such an avalanche of shame instantly and relentlessly on one person.

Empathy is understanding and sharing the feelings of another. Jesus didn't sympathize with the woman accused of adultery; He empathized with her. "Neither do I" means He shared every ounce of her suffering and shame.

God is a God of second chances who continually offers us His grace and mercy. Will we be courageous and empathetic and direct those who have sinned to God's forgiveness? Will we care when people lash out by using words of shame like stones, knowing we've all sinned and that one sin is no greater than the other? We've all come short and in thus doing almost missed the kingdom of God ourselves. We've all been blessed by God's grace and mercy through the redemptive blood of Jesus.

■ ■ ■

Begin today to recognize if you shame and bully others. Ask God for forgiveness and become a leader (especially online).

Journal

WEEK

10

Day 1

DAD'S HOUSE

"My Father's house has many rooms;
if that were not so, would I have told you that
I am going there to prepare a place for you?"

JOHN 14:2

She was eighteen years old and wanted me to meet her father. We left the prison-like orphanage and walked down the frozen streets in Moldova in Eastern Europe, where we had been filming all day. I was there with a film crew documenting the work of a ministry. It was spring and a freezing fifteen degrees.

When we reached her father's dilapidated cement house, she didn't knock. The door had no handle or lock, so we stepped down onto the floor of a dark dirt pit of a room. Her seventy-five-year-old father, who'd left her in the orphanage at the age of three never to return, sat in the middle of the room, toothless and dirty in front of an open fire. The house had no electricity or running water, and the only light came from a cracked and dirty window and the fire's glow.

She'd only met him when she had aged out of the orphanage at fifteen. She hugged him and gave him a bag of food, a bottle of water, and the blankets we'd brought. She was also just fifteen when she met her heavenly Father, who'd taught her how to forgive. She told me that she often imagines what kind of house her heavenly Father is preparing for her—them. Much of the world is bleak, but our Father has a place with beautiful rooms for us.

■ ■ ■

Stop and imagine God's house. Who will be there with you because your Father has forgiven you and in thus doing asked you to forgive those who wronged you.

Day 2

GOD'S DECOR

For I am convinced that neither death nor life, neither angels
nor demons, neither the present nor the future, nor any
powers, neither height now depth, nor anything else
in all creation, will be able to separate us from
the love of God that is in Christ Jesus our Lord.

ROMANS 8:38–39

*O*ur environment affects our mood and choices. I love holidays, so I decorate with seasonal décor. My family groans at my holiday boxes because I require their help with them, especially at Christmas. But I've also noticed how they groan when and the décor returns to the ordinary.

God had to take the children of Israel out of Egypt in order to save them. He also needed to change their environment and thus their perspective so they could fully embrace Him. But the Israelites weren't happy about it and there was much groaning. Even in the promised land, their sinful natures manifested. Eventually, those surroundings couldn't keep them from falling back into their old ways.

Even Paul struggled with bad choices. In Romans 7:19 he said, "For I do not do the good I want to do, but the evil I do not want to do—this I keep on doing." We all struggle and can't separate ourselves from sin. God may require us to change our surroundings. It's not until we're fully separated from our past and its tentacles of influence that we can see clearly its destructive impact and stay healthy and healed.

■ ■ ■

How do you need to change your environment to fully connect and live a changed life with God? Choose God's décor.

Day 3

BACK HANDING
SELF-CRITICISM

He says, "Be still, and know that I am God; I will be exalted
among the nations, I will be exalted in the earth."

PSALM 46:10

*P*rofessional tennis player Serena Williams said, "I guess it's
a part of being in the public eye. You have to accept that
people are going to have a say, whether it's your body, or your
face, or your hands. It could be your feet. Nothing is off limits.
I think that's why, growing up, my mum—not consciously, sub-
consciously—taught myself and all my sisters to be so strong. It
prepared me for these moments."[20]

Leaders and influencers know they have to squelch external
criticism, but especially internal criticism, if they're going to
succeed or they'll sabotage themselves and ultimately fail. As
fear increases, confidence and our ability to be resilient declines,
making it harder to learn from our failures. Consequently, we
continue to fail over and over again. So how do we deal with the
constant barrage of criticism?

God says, "Be still," and lift up His name. Jesus often left
the crowd to be alone and seek His Father's company. There He
found strength and peace to face the roaring and demanding
world. He then returned to the endless demands of the people
with renewed patience. He's our perfect peace and able to calm
anything that's volleyed at us in life.

■ ■ ■

How are you feeling defeated today? Stop and lift up His name in
praise. Let His peace propel your confidence over the line for a win-
ning season.

Day 4

DENT THE UNIVERSE

"But if serving the LORD seems undesirable to you,
then choose for yourselves this day whom you will serve,
whether the gods your ancestors served beyond
the Euphrates, or the gods of the Amorites, in whose
land you are living. But as for me and my household,
we will serve the LORD."

JOSHUA 24:15

*S*teve Jobs wanted to make a dent in the universe and do something historic, and he did when he founded Apple Inc. We all desire to leave our mark in this world, so we work hard to become great leaders, inventors, or parents, or perhaps to discover the cure for a disease.

Jesus also left a dent in the universe. He never wrote a theology book, created works of art, or life-changing tools and technologies, but He did bring us a cure. He cured our transgressions and shame and showed us how to live and thrive in this sinful world. Using the examples of real people and by telling parables, Jesus provided remedies. He made us think but allowed us to make up our own minds.

If you spend time with God, He'll ask you hard questions, but He'll always let you choose your own answer. Every day you're given a chance to make history with how you spend your time and live your life. Joshua gave the children of Israel a choice, but he chose the Lord. He is forever remembered for his leadership choices. What will yours be?

■ ■ ■

Who will you serve each day? How will your life dent the universe?

Journal

WEEK

11

Day 1

DESCENDANT WISDOM

We will not hide them from their descendants; we will tell
the next generation the praiseworthy deeds of the LORD,
His power, and the wonders He has done.

PSALMS 78:4

When my mom and dad passed on, I dug through their papers and searched their Bibles and journals looking for any thoughts and wisdom they might have left behind. I longed for one last connection, and those last bits of wisdom were all I had left to satisfy those longings.

Would your descendants be able to understand how God's truth and wisdom have affected your choices in life? Have you left them documentation of the awe of God's presence during your life journey—of how suffering and devastation challenged you but God saw you through it?

We have many technologies today—computers, iPads, blog posts, podcasts, and a myriad of ways to leave our faith and legacy for the next generation. Pencil and paper still work too. Instill the next generation with God's wisdom and knowledge from your life. Pass on how God's wonders and power transformed your heart and mind and brought purpose and contentment. We're thankful for the stories in the Bible that continue to teach and provide wisdom for us today. Don't hide yours from the next generation. Pen your praise for all He's done for you.

■ ■ ■

Write down a significant event or the milestones when God made a difference in your life. Don't forget to include those vulnerable moments. They make you human.

WALLS CAME TUMBLING DOWN

> You have broken through all his walls
> and reduced his strongholds to ruins.
>
> PSALM 89:40

*T*he Middle East government leader I was meeting for lunch on a sunny day in LA wanted to mobilize women using media, as she felt women would be a key to stopping terrorism. I had been asked by a global leadership group if I'd meet and explain how I integrate my faith with my work. Because in the Muslim culture, church and state are not separated.

She began the conversation by telling me that she'd been a traditional Muslim and had studied the life of Mohammad since birth but had never had dreams of him. Suddenly, she was having dreams of Jesus and she wanted to know about Him.

I have talked to others who have also spoken about Muslims coming to know Jesus through their dreams and visions. One new Muslim believer told of being in a mall in Dubai when a man came up to him and said that he'd had dreams of his face for three weeks and wanted to know why. The new believer then shared Jesus with the stranger.

God isn't using bullets and bombs to break down spiritual walls; He's using dreams and visions, and it's something He has done from the beginning of history. Read Daniel chapters 2 and 7, Matthew 1:20, and Acts 16:9 and 10:10. Even John recorded his visions in the book of Revelation. We need to be praying for God to send more dreams to those who are searching for Him so that ancient strongholds can be broken.

■ ■ ■

What stronghold has God broken down in your life? Pray that He will do the same for others.

Day 3

DEVOTION?
WHAT'S UP WITH THAT?

> "He will glorify me because it is from me that
> He will receive what He will make known to you."
>
> JOHN 16:14

*P*iety. It's an old word not often used today to define devotion to God. Some dictionaries call it a duty. In today's culture, piety is often based on what feels good—a hip pastor, rockin' worship music, and donuts in the church lobby. We've lost our perspective on what being a Christian requires.

God didn't send warm fuzzies when he confronted Moses and told him to lead thousands of people out of Egyptian bondage. Abraham wasn't skipping up the mountain with delight when God told him to sacrifice his only son. And don't get me started on the life and death of Jesus. These biblical examples weren't written to deter us from a godly life but to inspire us to live one.

How can we be truly devoted to God when it might be hard? We begin by magnifying Him. That means making Him bigger in our life. Jesus demonstrated this to us as He regularly retreated to be with God the Father in prayer. He knew it was essential to spend time with His Father. Piety means devoting your time to building an intimate relationship. It's out of your relationship that God brings clarity and endurance for the hard stuff in life. It's time for us to stop acting the part of a devoted follower of God and commit to it. He's called us to do big things, and they may be challenging, but it will be glorious. Glorify Him.

. . .

What does God want to make known to you, but you're avoiding because it doesn't feel good? How can you give it up and step into obedience?

DID YOU LEAVE THE DOOR OPEN?

Then Satan entered Judas, called Iscariot, one of the Twelve.

LUKE 22:3

When I was a kid, Mom and Dad were always repri- manding me for leaving the front door open. In Las Vegas, the summer heat often reached well over 100 degrees, so our air conditioner was constantly cranking. If the door was left open, the temperature in the house rose quickly—as did my parents' electric bill.

Likewise, many wrong choices in life happen without our noticing, and then we feel the heat and get the bill. Bad choices can start out as small leaks, but more often we leave the door wide open to them.

Judas Iscariot, one of Jesus' handpicked followers, chose to leave the door open and satan entered. But when did the small leaks begin in Judas's life? For God's plan to transpire, Jesus had to fulfill scriptural prophecy and die. He knew Judas's heart and nature, and He knew that even devoted hearts have natures that don't know how to keep doors shut to sin. Judas was an exam- ple of how easy it is to allow satan to enter our lives even when we know Jesus. This is why God never stops forgiving and His mercy is everlasting.

My parents never stopped loving me, nor did they abandon me for forgetting to shut the door. But I was justly punished. Did God forgive Judas? No one will know until we get to heav- en, but it cost Judas his earthly life.

■ ■ ■

What small leaks are drifting in under the door to your heart? Get some Jesus weather stripping—stay in prayer and His Word—and keep the door closed.

Journal

WEEK

12

Day 1

DIVERTED

Turn to me and be gracious to me,
for I am lonely and afflicted.
PSALM 25:16

*U*gh. I was diverted again, not off a Los Angeles freeway but from precious time with God.

I'd gotten up an hour early, but then I saw the laundry that hadn't gotten done the day before, so I took the time to throw it in the washing machine. After all, it could be washing while I prayed—right? Maybe I'd grab a cup of coffee for a sec. But there were the dishes still in the sink. Oh goodness, the trash truck was coming down the street, so I needed to get the garbage cans out too. And so it went. That extra time and those cherished moments of being wrapped in God's embrace before the day began had been stolen by my diverted eyes. Not on evil things, but on life's endless responsibilities. The guilt and frustration came screeching in like the high-pitched sound of wheels on the pavement just before the thud of a car wreck. How did I let that happen? Why didn't I notice the signs of diversion?

And then God's tender voice came softly rolling into my soul. The endless gracious ocean waves crashed and covered my anguished heart as He whispered, "You are loved with a deep and constant love, forgiven, embraced. I'm still here. Breathe in my fresh air, hear the beauty of the wind, and see the light of day." So I did.

■ ■ ■

What's getting in the way of your time with God? His everlasting love covers our diversions, and His grace is endless. How will you embrace Him today?

Day 2

DOING THE MOST
FOR THE LEAST

"The King will reply, 'Truly I tell you, whatever you did for one of
the least of these brothers and sisters of mine, you did for me.'"

MATTHEW 25:40

*T*he refugee crisis, with the massive exodus of Muslims and
Christians from war-torn regions in the Middle East, has
affected the world. I've had the privilege of traveling and connecting with some of the largest Christian churches around the
world, working with the leaders and pastors in many of these
regions and gaining firsthand information.

Finland and Sweden have been doing significant work. These
are cold-weather countries, but the refugees arrived wearing
shorts and sandals. The local Christians started with friendship—a truck serving coffee and tea—then brought clothing,
food, and medical assistance. Most importantly, they listened to
and loved the people. Now the once-vacant church buildings are
exploding with new Christian converts. The greatest need now
is leadership and Bible training. The refugees are hungry and
thirsty for the Word of God to fill their hearts and lives.

What the world sees as a crisis, God has turned into the
greatest of blessings in a strange twist of fate. Or was it the hand
of God? What seemed like a hopeless situation for the refugees
turned into their greatest gift—knowing the true and living
God. What the devil meant for evil, God turned to good. What
was least expected became more from God.

■ ■ ■

Who are "the least of these" in your community? Ask God to show you
what you can do to bring God's love to them.

Day 3

DON'T LET YOUR BABIES
BE COWBOYS

Start children off on the way they should go,
and even when they are old they will not turn from it.

PROVERBS 22:6

illie Nelson and Waylon Jennings, two iconic country music artists, recorded a duet of Ed and Patsy Bruce's song "Mamas Don't Let Your Babies Grow Up to Be Cowboys" in 1978. The words warn parents of the lifestyle of cowboys, who, according to the song, wander the range, are loners, and are hard to love.

God has instructed us to teach our children "the way they should go"—how to ride the range of life—so that when they're adults they won't "turn from it." But how are we to teach them when, as adults, we often don't even know the way to go?

Raising kids is a huge challenge, especially in our culture with its constantly forming potholes, which can quickly turn into sinkholes. It's a wild and dangerous life in the open range today. So, teach your children promise Scriptures and how to pray. Promise Scriptures are the rocks that fill in those potholes, and prayer is the cement that fill's the cracks, keeping the pavement smooth. They bring hope and restoration and will repair the damage done by the world's earthly erosion of sin and evil. Teach your children how to come in from the range and rest in God's green pastures found in His Word.

■ ■ ■

What promise Scriptures are you learning that you'll teach to your children? Start with this one.

Day 4

FASHIONING YOUR HEART

> "The LORD does not look at the things people look at. People look
> at the outward appearance, but the LORD looks at the heart."
>
> 1 SAMUEL 16:7

*S*alvation Army founder William Booth began taking church services to storefronts and the streets in London in the 1800s because poor people weren't allowed to attend churches. They couldn't afford the "proper" attire and many times even a bath. Years later, the Jesus Movement in the 1960s and 1970s brought yet another renewed understanding to the church, that putting restrictions on how people looked and dressed was keeping hippies away. God looks at the heart and not outward appearances. But do we need a fresh reminder of how to come into the sanctuary of God today?

Today, dressing down is trendy. Torn jeans and T-shirts are common high-dollar fashions. Many people never give a thought to what they or others are wearing to church. Until it *is* noticed. Until it becomes a reflection of our heart and attitude.

For some people, church has become a weekly event to socialize and listen to a great band. Do we think about the fact that we're entering God's sanctuary—the holy place of God's gathering of people? I wonder if we've lost something by not caring about how we show up or if we even show up on time? Are we preparing ourselves with our outward appearance to honor God and reflect our inward passion for Him? It's one thing if PJs are our best clothes, and another if we just don't care. Ultimately God doesn't care until you don't care about honoring Him.

■ ■ ■

How do you make church a priority? How does your outward appearance reflect your inward passion for Him?

Journal

WEEK

13

Day 1

DUPED

He also told them the parable: "Can the blind lead the blind?
Will they not both fall into a pit?"

LUKE 6:39

*C*razy Water, advertised as a miracle elixir, was bottled and sold in the early 1900s by its inventor, Ed Dismuke, who claimed it saved his life and could cure any ailment.[21] My father-in-law enjoyed a good joke and often sang the product's lively jingle to our kids. Could it fix any ailment? Probably not.

Have you ever been duped? I have. I've been talked into attending events, buying products, and eating things that I regretted. In today's media blitz and social-media culture, we can get duped quickly.

Overpacked schedules land us in pits that are often hard to climb out of, so I encourage you to take the time to check it out in God's Word. Surround yourself with trusted leaders and mentors, and get an additional opinion. Then continue to be open to the leading of the Holy Spirit. First John 4:1 instructs us, "Do not believe every spirit, but test the spirits to see whether they are from God, because many false prophets have gone out into the world." Then be cautious about what you post on the Internet. Let's be known as purveyors of truth. We live in a crazy world with waters unknown.

■ ■ ■

Have you ever been duped? How did you handle it and what did God teach you that you need to remember so you don't get duped again?

Day 2

EAGLE WINGS

Those who trust in the LORD will find new strength.
They will soar high on wings like eagles. They will run and
not grow weary. They will walk and not faint.

ISAIAH 40:31 NLT

I've been a victim of empty promises, struggles, and disappointments during my lifetime, and they never get easier. My husband, Phil Cooke, was honored to have been an executive producer on the Hillsong movie *Let Hope Rise*. Like all movies, it was a struggle to bring it to the screen. We had to live through the typical delays, but we were blindsided when the movie was thrown into a distribution crisis, causing a huge delay and additional issues before it was finally released.

The story of Ruth and Naomi in the Bible is all about waiting. Ruth said no to what seemed logical; she chose not to go back to her country and family. She decided to trust in a newfound God—the one of her deceased husband—and stick with a mother-in-law, Naomi, who was bitter over her situation and not much fun to be around. But Ruth's choices eventually brought her a great-grandson, King David. Out of her genealogy, Jesus would be born.

The world had waited for Jesus. He was our first great wait, and today we're waiting for His return. We need to "run and not grow weary" and "walk and not faint." Life is filled with the unexpected, but we have God's eagle wings.

■ ■ ■

What's one thing that you struggled to wait for, but the outcome has been a wonderful blessing? The next time you're waiting, remember this blessing and the Scripture above.

Day 3

ON THE PEAK WITH HOPE

"How beautiful on the mountains are the feet of those who
bring good news, ... who bring good tidings!"

ISAIAH 52:7

*T*he helicopter pilot dropped Joel Osteen and myself off on top of the mountain. Early in our careers, we were in Colorado filming a Christmas TV special for his father, Pastor John Osteen. My husband, Phil, and our camera operator stayed in the helicopter to film an epic opening shot of Pastor John standing on a snow covered peak high above a beautiful valley. Joel and I were there hiding in a snow bank behind a tree near his dad just in case of an emergency.

As the pilot took off, he yelled, "By the way, bears don't always stay hibernated. They can often wake up and are usually hungry, so keep an eye out. Also, I wouldn't go walking around much up here. The snow may look like it's solid, but you could drop down into a snow cave and be buried." Then he flew into the distance for the big shot. *Not a lot of hope in that warning*, we thought while we looked around for anything with teeth.

Well, we got the shot and survived.

Joel's messages are focused on *hope*. He and his wife, Victoria, have shared that message to millions worldwide. John and Dodie, Joel's parents, spent their lives in ministry, and Joel grew up witnessing God's power to change lives.

The fear of bears and snow caves couldn't deter Joel from the sure footing he's found in God's Word, because he knows where to run to.

■ ■ ■

Decide today that when you face the bears and snow caves of your life, you'll already know where to run—to Jesus.

Day 4

EFFERVESCENT ENSLAVEMENT

Never be lacking in zeal, but keep your
spiritual fervor, serving the Lord.

ROMANS 12:11

*O*verbooked. The airline was full, and someone was getting bumped if a volunteer didn't give up his or her seat. No one looked up or moved in the terminal; we all had places to go and things to do.

Often life gets old—not due to a lack of things to do, but because there's an overabundance. We overbook our lives with education, career, family, and everything we think will bring satisfaction and meaning to our lives. Then God asks us to give up our seat. *What? How can I miss that strategic career move? Did I hear God right? He wants me to go where? Volunteer? And give money that I saved for my well-deserved vacation? He wants me to give up (gulp) my life sacrificially to Him? And do it enthusiastically?*

Jesus did.

The Greek word for *servanthood* translates to "enslavement." Paul speaks from his experience—enslavement to Christ—when he tells us to guard our lives from burnout. We shouldn't lose our zeal—our effervescence, those bubbles of carbonation added to plain water to make it sparkle. When we make sacrifices, God brings bubbly contentment that can only come from obedience to Him. Stay alert and look for places to be an enthusiastic, fervent servant of God. Jesus enslaved Himself fully to God and volunteered His life. Can we give less?

■ ■ ■

Are you willing to take flight by being enslaved? Fasten your seatbelt and find a place to serve in God's kingdom. Write down three possible places where you could serve—then go.

Journal

WEEK

14

Day 1

END OF DISCUSSION

> As a father has compassion on his children, so the LORD
> has compassion on those who fear him; for he knows
> how we are formed, he remembers that we are dust.

PSALM 103:13–14

*L*eading child psychologists and parenting specialists advise parents to not allow children equal say in making decisions. A four-year-old isn't developmentally prepared to understand their needs and safety, like going to bed at a decent time or not playing in the street. A child's autonomy and feelings need to be balanced with structure, guidance, and empathy, and the rules of the parent don't always need to be explained. They exist for a purpose and need to be obeyed. It's not an issue of obedience but one of caring. Caring must be preeminent.

When we get angry and insist that God explain His discipline or seemingly deaf ear to our desires, we forget that His ultimate love for us takes precedence. We wonder why He doesn't answer our prayers, and question if He cares about our thoughts and desires. That's just it—He does care. He demands obedience because He knows us and knows our future. We're blinded by our immaturity and inability to understand our safety and needs. The Father is your friend, but He's your caring parent first. He'd rather you get angry, even cussing mad, than lose you or allow you to be put in harm's way.

■ ■ ■

What do you think God wants for you today? How does that compare to what you want? Keep in mind that He has your best interests in mind.

Day 2

ENDURANCE TEST

"You stiff-necked people! Your hearts and ears are
still uncircumcised. You are just like your ancestors:
You always resist the Holy Spirit!"

ACTS 7:51

*L*ife comes at us hard and it's not always fair. We want God to swoop in and save us at the last minute just like in the movies. But He doesn't work that way.

In Acts 7, Stephen addressed the Sanhedrin before being stoned as the first Christian martyr. He laid it all out, recalling the perils and trials from the time of Abraham. Life for the Jews (God's chosen people) had always been challenging, and they didn't recognize that Jesus had come to save them and bring restoration.

The Son of God has come to redeem us from the broken world we live in. Not the world He made for us, but the disastrous world we must now endure until His final return. He's *promised* us a new heaven and a new earth (Revelation 21:1), but His perfect time for this is not yet. One day He will relieve us of our suffering. Until then, Jesus is our Promise of a redeemed present and an indescribably wonderful future.

The question is, will we be strong enough to endure until He returns? Without a daily dose of His presence, we succumb to … well, life. God loves you deeply, and He wants you to thrive in this chaotic world. His will must come first though. When you draw close and know His ways, enduring this world becomes tolerable and joy comes swooping in.

■ ■ ■

Is your time with God rushed, or is it quality time? How could you deepen your relationship with Him?

Day 3

ENSLAVED

"I have the right to do anything," you say—but not
everything is beneficial. "I have the right to do anything"—
but I will not be mastered by anything.

1 CORINTHIANS 6:12

One of the interesting things about traveling the world regularly is reading about various international customs and laws. For example, it's illegal to bring chewing gum into Singapore. In India, a woman's exposed shoulders and ankles aren't unlawful, but they are disrespectful. In Muslim countries, a woman should have a scarf ready to cover her head. And many Jewish customs and laws can be traced back to the Old Testament, when they were practiced for health reasons.

But when Jesus came, He brought freedom from many of these laws and traditions, one of which was the slaughtering of a lamb for the redemption of our sinful nature. Jesus is the final lamb—the Lamb of God sacrificed to pay the price for our sin once and for all.

Giving humankind the freedom of choice has been a core desire of God from the beginning of time. Adam and Eve had choices and they made one big wrong one. We have many choices too. Marijuana, abortion, and euthanasia, for example, may be legal, but they may not be right or beneficial. Wrong choices enslave us, which leads to guilt and shame. God's choice is for us to be free from enslavement and anything that masters our heart and mind.

■ ■ ■

*What would you say is the master of your soul? If it's not God, what
do you need to do to make Him your Master?*

Day 4

ENTITLEMENT

> "From everyone who has been given much,
> much will be demanded; and from the one who has
> been entrusted much, much more will be asked."
>
> LUKE 12:48

I'm always around and mentoring many twenty- to thirty-year-olds who want to work in media and entertainment in Hollywood. We occasionally bring in media interns at our production company, and I've been an instructor at Biola University and presently teach for Asbury University. One of the issues I hear about from professors and employers is that many from the millennial generation seem to have an attitude of entitlement.

Recent college graduates often feel they deserve special treatment when entering the work place. Paying their dues and starting out at jobs they feel are beneath their qualifications is often something they scoff at. Most lack the humility and leadership skills that could get them to higher positions. Their parents have even complained to me about their inappropriate attitudes toward their work ethic, and I often also hear from large corporations who hire an additional HR person just to deal with parents complaining that their kids aren't promoted or treated fairly.

Attitude is everything. Especially when the competition in business today is intense. The reason many young people get passed over for a job is because of lack of humility and respect. How can young people stand out as Christians in today's competitive job market? By staying humble and having a servant spirit.

■ ■ ■

When was the last time you examined your attitude? Are you ready to lead humbly?

Journal

WEEK

15

Day 1

EQUIPMENT CHECK

Finally, be strong in the Lord and in his mighty power.
Put on the full armor of God, so that you can take your stand
against the devil's schemes. For our struggle is not against
flesh and blood, but against the rulers, against the authorities,
against the powers of this dark world and against the
spiritual forces of evil in the heavenly realms.

EPHESIANS 6:10–12

*W*hen I have gigs—media projects I've been hired to produce—and I'm setting up with the crew, we do multiple checks with cameras, lighting, and sound before rolling the camera. I often hire someone or put myself into the position of the person we'll be filming so the crew can practice with the equipment and be ready to shoot when the talent arrives. In the business we call this person a "stand-in." They are important people because they save money and time for the key talent and crew to be able to do their work.

God's wants your equipment—your armor—ready to go so that when He gives you an assignment, you won't fail but will stand up to the pressures of our modern culture's questions and issues. Do equipment checks by not being afraid to put yourself in biblical discussions. Research for yourself by reading magazines and blogs, and listening to theological arguments. Most importantly, keep your attitude in check, staying humble and caring, and be alert to spiritual forces that would deter you from your faith. You're standing in for Jesus on this earth and others are watching.

■ ■ ■

When have you delayed what God was calling you to do because you were unprepared? How can you check your equipment and be ready to take action the next time He calls?

Day 2

EQUIPPED

So Christ ... equip[ped] his people for works of service,
so that the body of Christ may be built up.

EPHESIANS 4:11–12

I hate buying a car. It's not that I'm ungrateful for the blessing of being able to own one, but it's the process—the game you have to play with car dealers—to get the best price. When buying a car, we all know that they come with standard equipment, and then for more money you can buy optional equipment. These are items deemed as luxury additions, but for many of us, they're needed if we want to drive in the climate and road conditions where we live.

We're born uniquely equipped by God. Then He further equips us according to His purposes and for what He desires us to achieve in life. Just as some of us live in desert places and need sand-appropriate tires and air conditioning, and others live in the mountains and need snow tires and good heaters, God brings into our lives the specific spiritual equipment we need. Sometimes it takes tearing out the old equipment and replacing it, which isn't always easy. How far we get down the road in life depends on our willingness to accept the equipment God needs to install for the journey He wants to take us on. Remember, His purposes are always for the building of His kingdom, and He will equip you with what you need.

■ ■ ■

What old equipment is God tearing out and changing in your life? Rejoice that the new replacements will be so much better and may take you on the journey of a lifetime.

Day 3

GOD'S PERFECT PACE

[May God] equip you with everything good
for doing His will, and may He work in us what
is pleasing to Him, through Jesus Christ,
to whom be glory for ever and ever. Amen.

HEBREWS 13:2

We don't like to be last. In today's fast-everything culture, being first rules. The problem is, how do we balance our culture's relentless drive to succeed and perform with God's often slower time table and His perfect will for our lives? It can be frustrating. God doesn't waiver from his agenda and what He wants to accomplish in us. Often in trying to keep up in a fast-paced lifestyle and career can cause us to miss God's perfect plan. In our impatience, we hastily make decisions or jet off in what we think is the direction God wants us to go until something happens and then we realize we went the wrong way. And we wonder why God is so far away?

It's the classic story of the tortoise and the hare. Both animals have merits, but only one wins. Or do they both? The contented tortoise won the race, but the hare learned a valuable lesson that the arrogance and laziness of his God-given abilities can result in being a loser. God blesses us with talents and abilities but expects us to respect the way He reveals His perfect plan to us. Ambition must be balanced with wisdom, and only God's sure and steady hand should be our guide.

■ ■ ■

At what race have you failed, even though you thought you were a sure winner? Write down where you momentarily lost your way. Ask Him to put you back in the right direction.

Day 4

THE AROMA OF KNOWLEDGE

> But thanks be to God, who always leads us as captives
> in Christ's triumphal procession and uses us to spread
> the aroma of the knowledge of him everywhere.
>
> 2 CORINTHIANS 2:14

The teenage girl was upset. It had been a hard day in middle school again, and that showed on her face when her mom picked her up after school. As they drove home, the mom glanced in the rearview mirror, wondering how she should broach the subject of what had happened this time. She kept seeing her daughter picking up the corner of her shirt, pulling it up to her nose, and smelling it over and over again. Perplexed by this odd behavior, the mom asked her what she was doing. "I'm smelling Daddy," she said. "He kisses me each morning, and his cologne stays on my clothing. When I'm in a tough situation, I smell my shirt and know he's with me. I'm not scared anymore."

Are you smelling the aroma of your heavenly Father when you're in a tough situation? He's right there with us and that knowledge is so captivating it can overpower difficult situations and allow us to live victoriously. Let His fragrance be a constant reminder that by trusting Him, His great provision, protection, and love can be made known to others.

■ ■ ■

What does the aroma of God's presence smell like to you? What knowledge of His great love could you share today so someone else could smell God's presence?

Journal

WEEK

16

EVE OF DESTRUCTION

> Since everything will be destroyed in this way, what kind
> of people ought you to be? You ought to live holy and godly
> lives as you look forward to the day of God and speed its
> coming. That day will bring about the destruction of the
> heavens by fire, and the elements will melt in the heat.
>
> 2 PETER 3:11–12

Years ago, P. F. Sloan wrote a bitter protest song, "Eve of Destruction," which was recorded by Barry McGuire. The opening verses tell of the Eastern world exploding, young killers toting guns, and bodies floating in the Jordan, as well as the "fear we all are feelin'." And that's just the first two verses. It was a scary song when it released in 1964, and it's even more so now as our world situations intensify.

Peter asked in the uncertain times he lived in, "What kind of people ought you to be?" We believe we live godly lives, but are we looking forward to the "eve of destruction"? Are we praying that God speeds it up? And how do we conduct ourselves in the meantime? Do we care about those who don't know that our final Hope is coming? Will we live our lives among the suffering and sacrificially give? Can we practice forgiveness and embellish ourselves with God's promises, standing in unwavering trust of His Word?

Let's not forget the second commandment Jesus taught us: "'Love your neighbor as yourself.'" (Mark 12:31). Are we on the eve of destruction? Only God knows.

■ ■ ■

How well do you know your neighbors and coworkers? Share Jesus with a couple of them today. We're on the eve of destruction.

Day 2

EVERGREEN TRUST

Those who trust in their riches will fall,
but the righteous will thrive like a green leaf.

PROVERBS 11:28

Las Vegas in the 1960s and 1970s was a unique and interesting place to grow up. From a tourist perspective, it's a city of glitz, glamour, and fast money. But I saw the ugly underbelly of the city—the devastation behind the bright lights of the Vegas Strip. Even today, the city still has the highest suicide rate in the country.[22] Trusting anything or anyone became a big hurdle for me because I had seen so much deception growing up. When I decided to trust God for my life, it was a big decision.

God continues to remind me that the bright lights of Vegas are a false promise of riches and fame. He's proven to me that the bright light of Jesus is the one and only true promise of security, contentment, and lasting peace. This world, with its promises of happiness, is not my final destination. The things I accumulate or any influence I attain due to my accomplishments will pass away, but my soul will thrive like a "green leaf" because of the redemption of Jesus and the grace of God.

■ ■ ■

Was there a time you fell victim to the allure of "bright lights"? Look closely at where you're putting your hope today. How can you stay evergreen?

Day 3

EXPAND YOUR SERVER SPACE

For now we see only a reflection as in a mirror;
then we shall see face to face. Now I know in part;
then I shall know fully, even as I am fully known.

1 CORINTHIANS 13:12

*W*e live in a visual culture, so being visually challenged today is getting harder as our world communicates using greater amounts visual content on our multitude of digital devices. Google-owned YouTube reported in 2012 that users watched 4 billion videos a day and spent 3 billion hours on their site each month. The site uploads sixty hours of video every minute, or one hour of video every second, and experts calculate that YouTube spends 4 million dollars per year just on server storage space alone.[23]

God would like to show us lots of things, but He can only download small bits of Himself and reveal partial plans that He has for us. As Christ followers who want to spend time regularly with Him, we choose how much we let Him control our hearts and minds. He waits for us to render ourselves to His will, resulting in our seeing only "in part" of what He wants to do in our lives. The glorious thing about serving God for many years is that He increases our server space every year. One day, my hope is that He'll be fully downloaded in my life so He can fully upload my soul to heaven.

■ ■ ■

What new things about Himself has God been showing you? What do you need to do so He can increase your server space with wondrous truths?

Day 4

EXPOSED BEAUTY

You are altogether beautiful, my darling;
there is no flaw in you.
SONG OF SOLOMON 4:7

God created a masterpiece when he created you. Just like Michelangelo chipped the stone away to reveal the statue of David, God wants to see you exposed and brought to life as a beautiful work of art. He sees a masterpiece, but has to do some chipping to let your inner beauty be seen.

We live in a culture of "not enough." The addiction to always wanting more began with Adam and Eve. Satan convinced Eve she needed more, so she bit into the fruit of the Tree of Knowledge of Good and Evil and convinced Adam he needed more. They'd had it all. They were masterpieces but thought they weren't good enough. Satan convinced them of it.

Has the deceiver convinced you that you need more things to be seen and noticed by the world's standards? Those standards are satan's deceptions. God may have to chip away that worldly stuff, so don't fret when His gentle taps are felt. He's opening you up so your inward beauty is seen.

Adam and Eve's punishment was separation from God. Jesus gave His life so God could fix our sin-encrusted lives. It's the inward stuff—our souls—that will last for eternity. How do you want to end up—exposed forever as God's masterpiece or hidden in stone forever doomed?

■ ■ ■

What worldly "stuff" are you letting get in the way of the work God wants to accomplish in you? How can you let God remove it?

Journal

WEEK

17

Day 1

FACING THE FIRE

> "My people come to you, as they usually do, and sit
> before you to hear your words, but they do not put
> them into practice. Their mouths speak of love,
> but their hearts are greedy for unjust gain."
>
> EZEKIEL 33:31

In today's culture, we've compromised Scripture to make it politically correct. I was thinking about that on a recent visit to Oxford University, where I came across the often-overlooked Martyr's Memorial. It's a testament to three men—Anglican bishops Hugh Latimer and Nicholas Ridley and the Archbishop of Canterbury, Thomas Cranmer—who were burned at the stake in 1534 by Queen Mary Tudor for standing up for truths written in the Bible.

Cranmer's part of the story is particularly dramatic. He was a leader in the Church of England, and had annulled King Henry VIII's marriage to Catherine of Aragon, Mary's mother, so Henry could marry Anne Boleyn. The bishops had embraced Protestant teachings, but when Mary took the crown, she had them convicted of heresy in her attempt to restore the Catholic church in England. Cranmer tried to save himself by recanting his Protestant beliefs and then "recanted his recant." Mary had him burned anyway. As the fire lapped at his feet, he reached down so the flames would burn his right hand first and proclaimed, "I have sinned, in that I signed with my hand what I did not believe with my heart."[24]

■ ■ ■

What truth have you compromised (or considered compromising) to gain popularity? How can you keep your beliefs grounded in the Bible?

Day 2

FEEL THE BURN, PASS ME JESUS

Be joyful in hope, patient in affliction, faithful in prayer.

ROMANS 12:12

*M*an, that hurts. How could that have happened to me? Ever think those words because of either physical or emotional pain? Our culture moves with lightning speed toward what looks like a sure thing and the perfect end game. Then somehow the rug gets pulled, the ball is dropped, and the pain of defeat is imminent. Can you still be joyful in God's hope, patiently trusting His will, and faithful in consistent prayer?

God has a perfect plan set forth for you and this planet, but it may be painful at times. Can you trust Him when it really hurts? And what do you do in the meantime? Well, you look for new ways to love, trust, and serve Him *more* in all you're called by Him to do. You get creative and look for ways to be inventive and innovative.

The reward is stronger faith. You experience Him more when it's painful. It seems unnatural and even odd how He works, but that's why God's so thrilling. He has mysteries and plans for you that you've never dreamed could happen. Can you be a bold warrior of faith? God has a remedy for life's painful situations, but sometimes you have to feel the burn first. He's there in the midst, bringing healing with a peace unlike anything this logical world can comprehend.

■ ■ ■

How are you feeling the burning touch of Jesus? He has pain-killing promises in His Word. Find one and memorize it.

FINE-TUNED

The LORD is close to the brokenhearted
and saves those who are crushed in spirit.

PSALM 34:18

"I'm fine!" That's the pat answer for, "Don't bother me. I don't want to engage." It's a two-word cultural pleasantry, but it's a lie. We're never *just fine*. Maybe it's because we don't want to engage with the painful truth of our soul. But we'll never heal and be the authentic people God calls us to be until we do.

One of the beautiful aspects of accepting our brokenness is that we can then recognize and care for others in their brokenness. If we dam up the stream of God's love and forgiveness, we become hidden, isolated people. God calls us to be a community of believers that shares burdens and works together so His kingdom flourishes. When we allow God to fine-tune our life, beautiful music happens. An orchestra of messed-up people are joined together and make a distinctive triumphal sound. Each person has a unique instrument—a story of grace that makes angelic music that lifts up the name of Jesus.

We're all a mess, but God heals our out-of-tune lives and creates symphonies. He intends for us to live not in perpetual brokenness but in realms of rapturous music never before heard.

■ ■ ■

What do you say when people ask how you are? How are you a broken string that God is fine-tuning?

Day 4

ATTENTIVE

The eyes of the LORD are on the righteous,
and his ears are attentive to their cry.

PSALM 34:15

I remember thinking about God's godly servants as I sat on a train in Peru headed to historic Machu Picchu. I had just come from a global conference in Lima for ministers and marketplace leaders who were doing significant kingdom work. Many had been on the frontlines of assisting the floods of refugees pouring into their countries. They hadn't been prepared for the overwhelming needs, and they also hadn't been prepared for how God met them and His outpouring of the Holy Spirit as thousands came to know Jesus. These incredibly humble and gifted leaders dealt with each endless problem, bringing God's hope to those who had lost everything.

Sitting on the train that day, I also remember watching peasant farmers clearing a field next to the train with the help of a cow, using only hand tools. It was so tranquil and such a beautiful spring day. No one knew then that in only a few days, the nearby river would swell and become a raging force of devastation as torrential rains would bring the worst flooding in years to the region. Many people were swept away and killed, but God was still attentive. Whether in devastating wars or natural disasters, He always hears our cry.

■ ■ ■

What floods are you experiencing in your world? No matter what's happening, God sees His righteous people and knows what they're going through. What miracle are you expecting from Him today?

Journal

WEEK

18

THE TIMES THEY ARE
A-CHANGIN'

"I the LORD do not change.
So you, the descendants of Jacob, are not destroyed."

MALACHI 3:6

The 2016 Nobel Peace Prize recipient, singer/songwriter Bob Dylan, wrote the song "The Times They Are A-Changin'" in 1964 not knowing how the Internet and our media would affect cultural change so quickly in the twenty-first century. We can't keep up with the instantaneous changes we're confronted with in our daily lives. We're enamored with what's trending, and the overabundance of information coming at us instills even greater fear than ever before in our history. Information doesn't always bring knowledge, understanding, or peace.

God said He never changes. His Word and eternal plan for mankind won't waver either. As believers, He compels us to stand on His promises and "lean *not* on [our] own understanding" (Proverbs 3:5). We're the descendants of Jacob, and we will not be destroyed or lost, and that's a promise. We're secure in Him, and God repeatedly tells us in Scripture to not fear and to stay alert, using godly wisdom as we navigate the seas of constant change.

The times may be changing at light speed, but God's Word is firm. Stay confident as you check in with the news and events of the world each today. God's ultimate plans prevail.

■ ■ ■

What confident Scriptural promise will you hide in your heart today? How will you let it change or not change the decisions you make?

Day 2

FORGET-ME-NOT BIBLE STORIES

For He issued His laws to Jacob; He gave His instruction to
Israel. He commanded our ancestors to teach them to their
children, so the next generation might know them—even
the children not yet born—and they in turn will teach their
children. So each generation should set its hope anew on God,
not forgetting His glorious miracles and obeying His commands.

PSALM 78:5–7 NLT

*O*nce upon a time … Let me tell you a story … These opening
lines grab our attention because our nature connects to
stories. Yet with all the love we have for them, somehow we
don't teach them to our children and grandchildren. In today's
blockbuster-movie culture, the stories of the Bible are being
overshadowed and replaced by Hollywood versions. After all,
they are all *stories*—right?

Wrong. The trustworthy accounts of the Bible have lived
on for thousands of years, and they are not myths or legends.
They're biblical history, and we need to teach them to our children today so they recognize the evidence and wisdom of God.
Our culture is bombarding us with contrasting media and entertainment stories, so take the time and make it a priority to
teach children historical and trustworthy Bible stories.

Your journey with God matters too. Have you told your
children the story of your journey with God and what He's
taught you? The wisdom and faith you leave could be a catalyst
for loved ones in the future and for their eternity.

■ ■ ■

*What is your favorite Bible story, and why? Write down what it
taught you so you can pass it on to your children.*

112

Day 3

FORGIVENESS GRENADES

The weapons we fight with are not the weapons
of the world. On the contrary, they have
divine power to demolish strongholds.

2 CORINTHIANS 10:4

I've attended the Sundance Film Festival many times and it's always interesting. One year I viewed a film that heavily attacked Christians. Oftentimes, harsh and unkind treatment by Christians towards the LGBT community has created hate and rejection, and regrettably, that's cut off intelligent, gracious dialogue and often caused irreparable injury.

The creators of the film came forward after the screening for Q and A, to be greeted by an audience that was enraged by the evils of Christianity. After several questions about how the film was produced, the story that led to its making, and how the writer/director had been injured by Christians, one of the Christian producers I was with boldly stood to address the audience. He confessed to being a Christian and then humbly, almost tearfully, apologized for what the Christian community had done to the writer/director. He asked, as a Christian, to be forgiven.

Suddenly the room's anger deflated and a pin drop could be heard. The writer/director began to cry and said that the producer was the first Christian who had ever apologized to him.

Forgiveness grenades explode strongholds of hate and destroy situations of satan's destruction. We need to use them willingly and often.

■ ■ ■

Who do you need to forgive today? Look for places to launch a few forgiveness grenades.

FOUL TASTE

> "So, because you are lukewarm—neither hot nor cold—
> I am about to spit you out of my mouth."
>
> REVELATION 3:16

I'm not a fan of room temperature water. I often call myself an "ice-aholic" because I love ice cubes so much. If it's hot outside, room temperature water doesn't quench my thirst. Likewise, if it's freezing cold, I want my coffee and tea blazing hot.

God has issues with apathetic, uncommitted believers—ones that cling to Him only when there's a crisis or it's convenient. He also has issues with those who are conceited—the uppity believers who are legalistic and judgmental. Revelation 3:17 continues with, "But you do not realize that you are wretched, pitiful, poor, blind and naked." Both types of people, complacent and smug, aren't hot or cold (which are useful temperatures) but are lukewarm—good for nothing. They're thick-skinned, bitter individuals who are so self-assured and self-righteous that God finds them useless.

When we are neither hot or cold, we lose our unique usefulness. God even calls us "bitter" and will spit us out. It's easy to be distasteful in our culture today. It takes determination and a godly mind-set to be kind committed Christians and to be useful and healthy for God's kingdom.

■ ■ ■

What actions of yours would leave a bitter taste in God's mouth? How could you change them? Read the entire chapter of Revelation 3 where John talks about "gold refined by fire" that's never rejected.

Journal

WEEK

19

Day 1

SPIRITUAL BREAD

I have been young, and now am old, yet I have not seen
the righteous forsaken or his children begging for bread.
PSALM 37:25 ESV

At the turn of the twentieth century, my grandmother and grandfather immigrated to America due to devastating poverty and famine in France. They had to make the choice of either dying if they stayed or possibly dying by trying to escape. They knew hunger and famine, and never forgot the pain they felt when they had nothing to eat. For this reason, they taught me how to stay nourished but with more than physical food.

Our souls also need spiritual food. In John 6:35, Jesus said that He was the "bread of life" and that if we believed in Him, we'd never be thirsty or hungry. He knew that if we starved ourselves by not praying and reading our Bibles, our souls would be malnourished. And that we'd binge eat on "junk food"—the enticements of the world that we think will satisfy our soul's longings but still leaves us empty and craving for more.

It's only the bread of heaven that can keep us healthy and fit to face the uncertainties of a chaotic and unpredictable world.

■ ■ ■

What "eating" habits do you need to change? Ask God to feed your soul, and eat till your heart's content.

Day 2

FRUITCAKES

Jesus said to him, "Today salvation has come to this house,
because this man, too, is a son of Abraham.
For the Son of Man came to seek and to save the lost."

LUKE 19:9–10

*F*ruitcakes have been joke Christmas gifts in America for years. We laugh, but at one time they were given with much love and thought. These desserts have been eaten since the Roman era and were made popular because of their ability to be preserved and eaten over long periods of time.

People often call those who have odd or irritating personalities a "fruitcake." But there aren't any fruitcakes in the eyes of God. Our culture has made it easy to dismiss strange people rather than take the time to engage with them and, when appropriate, share God's love and message of redemption. God made us unique for His purposes. His salvation is for everyone no matter what they've done or how strange they seem to us.

In Hollywood, I'm often around offbeat artists, but I've learned that many people we consider odd are highly intelligent and quite interesting. They look at life differently and have insights I've never thought about in many ways. So next time, don't pass on the fruitcakes that come your way; they might bring a rich and sweet new perspective to your life if you stay open and willing.

■ ■ ■

When have you avoided someone who's odd? Ask God how you can see His creation through the eyes of Jesus. He preserves us for His purposes, and we're all valuable.

Day 3

GROANS FOR HOPE

> In the same way, the Spirit helps us in our weakness.
> We do not know what we ought to pray for, but the Spirit
> himself intercedes for us through wordless groans.
>
> ROMANS 8:26

*T*he "terrible twos" must be overwhelmingly frustrating for children, and in God's graciousness, most of us don't remember that age. A two-year-old's brain is awakening to life around them, but they're unable to communicate fully with words. Frustration and sometimes tantrums result. But while two-year-olds find relief in time, those with Locked-in syndrome must live out their days paralyzed and unable to communicate (except possibly with their eyes). The 2007 Oscar-nominated film *The Diving Bell and the Butterfly* is the true story of *Elle* magazine's editor, Jean-Dominique Bauby, who succumbed to the disease.

Often, we're locked in, in our spiritual life. Unable to verbalize the pain and suffering, we grunt and cry out to God. Mounting issues come at us in life, and they can keep us from seeing clearly or functioning reasonably. So the Holy Spirit graciously intercedes, interprets our heart's cry, and rescues us. Our groans are heard and understood by the Father.

When you're about to fall off a cliff, or you feel locked in due to bad choices or just unrelenting life issues, remember that your mind and heart still work. Groan. God understands, and He's there bringing hope.

■ ■ ■

What situation has locked you in and left you unable to pray? When that happens, cry out with your heart. The Holy Spirit will interpret for you.

Day 4

GAME OF DESIRE

But I say, walk by the Spirit, and you will not carry out the
desire of the flesh. For the flesh sets its desire against the Spirit,
and the Spirit against the flesh; for these are in opposition to
one another, so that you may not do the things that you please.

GALATIANS 5:16–17 NASB

At the Sundance Film Festival several years ago, I watched a documentary about the effects of online gaming on children and young adults. The film focused on Asian cultures that are immersed in it. The addictive tentacles of these video games are strangling families—and not just in Asia. It's a global issue. Many distraught and desperate parents are taking their children to rehab facilities and counselors for help. In the documentary, teens were ditching school and often wouldn't stop to bathe or eat. Most had stopped communicating with family and friends, preferring to spend days in a dark room, captivated by a video screen.

Video gaming is only one example of how satan attacks our souls with our desires. So how can we put up shields against the demonic bullets being fired at us daily? We stay close to the Holy Spirit, keeping our heart's desire focused on spiritual engagement. It's never going to be easy, but it will always be an essential one in today's culture of easy entrapment. In today's onslaught of media and online enticements, be on guard for subtle deceptions and how you're spending your time. Ephesian 6:16 says, "In addition to all this, take up the shield of faith, with which you can extinguish all the flaming arrows of the evil one." Examine where and how you're spending your time.

■ ■ ■

How has satan been shooting his bullets at you? What Scripture can you memorize today as your shield against him?

Journal

WEEK

20

Day 1

GATHER TOGETHER

And let us consider how we may spur one another on
toward love and good deeds, not giving up meeting together,
as some are in the habit of doing, but encouraging
one another—and all the more as you see
the Day approaching.

<small>HEBREWS 10:24–25</small>

I believe "the Day" is approaching when Jesus will return for His believers. And media is going to play a huge part. That's why regular gatherings of like-minded Christians are essential. While the Internet church and live-streamed church services are growing fast, regular physical gatherings encourage us to build our faith as a community.

As a media consultant, I encourage the use of multiple media platforms to propel those on the fringe of belief to "taste and see that the Lord is good" (Psalm 14:8). But when visitors attend a brick-and-mortar church, they need to engage with a welcoming face because live gatherings are where God's hope is seen and felt in worship and Word.

Time is a precious commodity in our culture, and choosing to be a part of a community of believers is time well spent. However, with packed schedules the ability to attend a church service online can be a welcome option when needed. Don't be afraid to engage via media, but get yourself to a gathering of believers regularly. Community matters.

■ ■ ■

In what ways are you isolating yourself from other Christians? Renew your commitment to gather with other believers.

123

Day 2

GET A LIFE

Then he said to his disciples,
"The harvest is plentiful but the workers are few."

MATTHEW 9:37

Over the years, I've been privileged to be able to direct successful Christian conferences, and have spoken at many.

All conferences need reliable volunteers, but finding them is always a challenge. In our busy lives with jam-packed schedules, time is our most valued currency and working at a conference may not seem valuable. Volunteering isn't about fulfilling a job, but about learning how to serve. When we're subjected to others' personalities, leadership styles, and work habits, we experience how the body of Christ functions and flourishes under grace. Attitudes have to be checked at the door.

Volunteering is about investing in someone else's life. In our culture today, we can get distracted by insignificant things because we've centered our lives on ourselves. We gain God's greatest blessings when it's personally challenging and inconvenient. Conferences are about learning new things, but I've experienced and seen others learn even greater lessons from working behind stage doors. God brings knowledge and wisdom when we're confronted with issues and personalities that are foreign to us. Let God teach you how to be a leader by being a servant.

■ ■ ■

What are some places you could volunteer and give of your life? What's holding you back, and how can you remedy that?

Day 3

WALK ON WATER

"Lord, if it's you," Peter replied, "tell me to come to you
on the water." "Come," he said. Then Peter got out of
the boat, walked on the water and came toward Jesus.

<small>MATTHEW 14:28–29</small>

In one of the classic scenes in the iconic film *Jaws*, Chief
Brody is sitting on the beach, transfixed on what could be
in the water and not on the beautiful sunny day or the people
having fun. When he spots a shark fin above the surface of the
water, fear grips him. Without hesitating, he bolts out of his
chair to clear the crowds from the water.

When the storm came up on the Sea of Galilee, Peter must
have had that kind of focus on Jesus as he stepped out of a perfectly good boat. Notice in this Scripture, he didn't get out immediately but waited until he was sure it was Jesus. He waited
to hear the Master's voice. When Jesus said, "Come," Peter bolt-
ed. All natural fear was shattered and Peter stepped into God's
nature—the supernatural ways of God.

Peter focused his eyes on the miraculous power of Jesus,
then took his eyes off Jesus and sank. God may be asking you to
do something daring that requires His supernatural help. Chief
Brody was called to kill a big fish. God wants us to focus on
Him, listen for His voice, and then bolt—stepping out into life's
challenges.

■ ■ ■

*Is God asking you to walk on water? Keep focusing on Him and lis-
tening for His voice. Write down what He's saying to you so you don't
forget His lessons and take your eyes off Him.*

Day 4

YOU SNOOZE, YOU LOOSE

"Whoever tries to keep their life will lose it, and whoever loses
their life will preserve it. I tell you, on that night two people
will be in one bed; one will be taken and the other left."

LUKE 17:33–34

I clearly remember traveling to summer camp when I was
a child, singing "Oh You Can't Get to Heaven" with a bus
full of loud and silly kids. It was a great traveling song because
each line was followed by an echo and there were so many verses it kept us occupied during the long trip. Each verse detailed a
way we couldn't get the heaven—on roller skates, in a rocking
chair, on our mother's apron strings, and on and on.

Fun and games aside, there will come a time when we'll all
stand before God. Alone. If you've heard God's inner voice in
your soul, it's time to make a clear choice about the direction
you want to journey in life. Will you confess that you aren't
enough to make it to heaven without God's grace and the redemption of Jesus, or will you be left guessing if there's a better
way to save your soul and make it to heaven? You can't go to
heaven on your mother's—or anyone else's—faith either. It has
to be your own decision to repent and your own relationship to
the living God. Romans 3:23 says, "For all have sinned..."

The deceiver—the devil—tells us it's not fun or fulfilling
when we give up our life and surrender it to God and that life
will be boring and irrelevant. But I've found just the opposite.
Have you tried Him? Or are you holding onto something else?

■ ■ ■

*What's keeping you from knowing God intimately? If you're not sure,
ask God and see what answer He gives.*

Journal

WEEK

21

Day 1

GODLY DIGESTION

"So the last will be first, and the first will be last."

MATTHEW 20:16

As a kid, I always thought it was odd when my dad ate his salad last at dinnertime, a habit he learned from his immigrant French heritage. But health experts tell us that we actually should be eating our greens at the end of our meal. When we eat green salads first, as most Americans do, we actually slow down food digestion. My dad always winked and told us that he was saving the best for last.

Jesus walked with His disciples for three years, teaching them new and sometimes odd ways of looking at—or digesting—life. He challenged their thinking and what they'd been taught, often against the norm. But I believe He kept His greatest teaching for the Last Supper. He didn't teach them when to eat salad but how to give sacrificially and that by being last, they were first in God's eyes. He demonstrated this by washing their dirty, stinky, travel-worn feet.

Jesus knew exactly what was coming in the next days, and if anyone deserved a pleasant and pampered meal, He did. Yet He lowered Himself to the lowest of servants and showed His followers how they should serve. Using the parable of the workers in the vineyard (Matthew 20:1–16), he taught about unfairness and being willing to accept what's been handed to us. Because life doesn't always go down the way we think. God may ask us to digest things differently.

■ ■ ■

Has something happened in life that you thought was unfair? How can you practice godly digestion?

Day 2

GODLY ENTRY

You have searched me, LORD, and you know me.
You know when I sit and when I rise; you perceive my
thoughts from afar. You discern my going out and my lying
down; you are familiar with all my ways. Before a word is
on my tongue, you, LORD, know it completely.

PSALM 139:1–4

I was exhausted from traveling but took off walking fast through the Los Angeles International Airport. Getting through customs after a long plane trip is always challenging, and my plane was one of several that had just landed, so hundreds of people were descending on the customs desks. At that moment, I thanked God I could fast-track the reentry process with "Global Entry." While it had been a long process of paperwork, interviews, and exposing to the government private information to get approval, avoiding the huge lines was worth it.

God knows us, formed us, but He wants godly entry to our souls. He wants unrestricted access to our hearts and minds. In order for that to happen, we must expose our intimate selves to Him. Interestingly, He knows our details, but He waits for us to open ourselves to His will. It's our choice as to how long we want to make the process, and even once we begin the application of His truths in our lives, it may take years before we finally allow Him to have complete entry. But it's so worth it.

■ ■ ■

How much entry to your soul have you allowed God? Divulge your life to Him and take the fast track to a life that flourishes.

Day 3

GOOD EQUIPMENT

Now may the God of peace … equip you with everything
good for doing his will, and may he work in us what is
pleasing to him, through Jesus Christ, to whom be
glory for ever and ever. Amen.

HEBREWS 13:20–21

One of the biggest and truly amazing retail chains in the United States is Bass Pro Shops. Resembling small museums, the stores are designed with giant aquariums and taxidermized animals. They sell endless varieties of hunting and outdoor sporting equipment, allowing customers to gear up for adventure in just about any place in the world.

God also wants to take us on adventures to overcome evil with good (Romans 12:21). But we will need good equipment and He alone knows our unique needs. He has called each of us to go do different things for His purposes. Are you shopping at His storehouse before you go? Explore the Bible for your godly equipment needs. Observe His creation. Nature has lots to teach us about how God provides and protects for us. God's amazing riches allow us to gear up for the spiritual adventure He's waiting to take us on.

So gather your supplies of grace, forgiveness, and long-suffering. And don't forget to bring along His defense Scriptures to keep you from evil perils. Pleasing God is our final destination.

■ ■ ■

What specific item do you need from God's storehouse? How fortunate we are that all the supplies are free and His doors are open 24/7/365.

Day 4

GOOD FATIGUE

And let us not be weary in well doing:
for in due season we shall reap, if we faint not.

<small>GALATIANS 6:9 KJV</small>

*D*uring a 2017 airing of the TV news show *CBS Sunday Morning*, rock star Lady Gaga said that home is the only place she can be herself and rest; when she leaves her home and crosses the property line, from that point on, she belongs to the public. Elvis suffered deep depression and insomnia, as did Marilyn Monroe, and both ended their lives by overdosing on drugs. They had brought smiles to thousands, but even our passions and talents can make us weary.

I'm on the national board for the Salvation Army, whose motto is "Doing the Most Good." To keep themselves ready for disasters and the needs of others, and do the "most good," Salvation Army volunteers and officers know they need to keep strict schedules that require periods of rest. Even God rested on the seventh day.

When we get tired, we get grouchy and can make bad decisions. In our culture of endless schedules and the convenience of technologies that allow us to take our work home, we need to remember that God wants us to shut down and rest. If we don't, mistakes will happen, poor choices will be made, and relationships will suffer. Faint not. Be willing to stop.

■ ■ ■

When was the last time one of your must-dos became your undoing? What could you adjust in your schedule to make more time for rest in your life?

Journal

WEEK

22

Day 1

GRACIOUS ACTS

> Do nothing out of selfish ambition or vain conceit. Rather,
> in humility value others above yourselves, not looking to your
> own interests but each of you to the interests of the others.
>
> PHILIPPIANS 2:3–4

*A*t the 2017 Grammy Awards, Adele won both Album of the Year and Song of the Year. The media had revealed great competition between her and Beyoncé, and observers were watching how it would play out.

Most winning artists are gracious in thanking producers, engineers, agents, and others who have contributed to the success of their projects, but Adele went out of her way to recognize Beyoncé's work—so much so that social media sites lit up, criticizing Adele for not giving herself credit for her own talent and accomplishments. I'm unfamiliar with Adele's spiritual life, but I do know that her graciousness was an example of selflessness to all who were watching.

Are we valuing others in the workplace and considering our competition enough to acknowledge their accomplishments? Are we being gracious, perhaps even helpful, so others can succeed? We live in a highly competitive world and need to let others see God's heart and graciousness though our unselfish acts. Let's be known and maybe even criticized for being overly gracious. Let's be known as Christians who are endlessly unselfish and forever giving.

■ ■ ■

Who are you competing with right now? What kind act of giving can you do for them? Send them a note of encouragement or perhaps an insider tip that might be insightful.

Day 2

HARD-PRESSED

[Jesus] fell with his face to the ground and prayed,
"My Father, if it is possible, let this cup be taken from me.
Yet not as I will, but as you will."

MATTHEW 26:39

*B*eing the granddaughter of French immigrants, winemaking was part of my upbringing. My brother and I inherited several winemaking tools and bottles, as well as a keen interest in the process. One of the crucial parts of winemaking is the pressing of the grapes.

Gethsemane was like a winepress for Jesus. He was being torn, squeezed, and pressed for our eternal lives. Jesus was new wine that God the Father was bringing forth to the world. The Bible goes on to say that Jesus literally sweated blood from his pores. His crucified life brought forth eternal life.

Jesus commanded His disciples to pray that night. Sounds simple, right? They still failed. Jesus, disappointed, found His followers asleep. Have you been asleep too? God's called us to intoxicate the world with His new wine and tell the story of the redemption of Jesus. When you're hard-pressed into a situation, it's time to get up, pray, and stay alert. Pray, the way Jesus taught us to pray: "Your will, Father, not mine."

■ ■ ■

What pressures of life are squeezing you right now? What Scripture can you memorize today to stay alert?

Day 3

GOD SO LOVED

For God so loved the world that he gave
his one and only son, that whoever believes in him
shall not perish but have eternal life.

JOHN 3:16

This verse is one of the most quoted Scriptures today, but we race through it so often that we've lost its most significant four words: "so loved … He gave."

Jesus came from heaven to earth and encased Himself in human skin. He was fully human and fully God. In Jesus' humanity, God gave Him the ability to choose—and Jesus chose to fully give. He loved so much that He endlessly gave. Everything He did on earth centered on His giving to the final end, when He gave His life so we could have life eternal.

The act of giving is preached relentlessly by followers of Christ. Unfortunately, many only associate it with giving money. Our selfishness is like cement walls around our hearts and minds, keeping love from breaking down the walls of evil that can impact the world. Giving is the beginning of joy and a mystery of God that can only be experienced when it's done with love.

■ ■ ■

How can you "so love" others and give outrageously? How might that get the attention of unbelievers?

Day 4

HEAD BOBS

Pray also for me, that whenever I speak,
words may be given me so that I will fearlessly
make known the mystery of the gospel …

EPHESIANS 6:19

I've been privileged to take several trips to India. One of the charming characteristics of the Indian people is the way they bob their heads—an almost circular motion of the head that sways right to left and then around several times quickly. They seem to do this unconsciously when undecided or thinking, and often out of kindness because they don't want to say yes or no and disappoint you. They also bob their head in place of verbally saying thank you. They are an extremely respectful culture.

Speaking the language of the culture must have been especially hard as Paul traveled to foreign lands. As a speaker whose has traveled to many different countries to speak myself, I know the many challenges and I'm thankful for translating apps on my smartphone to assist me today. Paul was a great leader and speaker for Jesus but admitted he was human and fearful and still had to pray for courage. I imagine he might have done some head bobs from time to time, but His love for God's people was always apparent in his messaging. We need to make sure there is love and respect wherever and whenever we are called to share the gospel.

■ ■ ■

How are you communicating God's messages to the culture you live in? Respect and love is always the key and maybe a head bob or two.

Journal

WEEK

23

Day 1

HEALING THE SEVERED

When Jesus heard what had happened, he withdrew by boat
privately to a solitary place. Hearing of this, the crowds followed
him on foot from the towns. When Jesus landed and saw a large
crowd, he had compassion on them and healed their sick.

MATTHEW 14:13–14

In Budapest, Hungry, they have a famous museum in a building that was first used by Nazis and then Communists as a prison and interrogation facility. Inside is a room they used for torture. It has an iron door in front of a tiny space—just big enough for you to stand. When the door slams shut, you're standing in the dark, entombed and unable to lift your hands to scratch your nose, which hopefully didn't get broken when the door slammed shut. The creative imagination of our twisted minds for torture is truly baffling.

John the Baptist, the cousin of Jesus and the one who baptized Him in the Jordan River, was arrested, put in prison, and beheaded. His severed head was then placed on a platter and presented to Herod's devious, vicious wife.

Jesus loved John dearly, and the news of his torture and sacrificial death must have been heartbreaking. But Jesus didn't seek revenge from the crowds that followed Him. He forgave. He didn't allow this tortuous act to cause people to stumble; instead, He taught them forgiveness and healed them. Likewise, God brings healing to our unjust situations—those inhumane places we're put into, where our heads may be physically severed but never our hearts.

■ ■ ■

What do you need to forgive another for? Write down your sufferings, forgive, and let God heal you.

141

Day 2

HEALTHY FORGIVENESS

"The LORD is slow to anger, abounding in love
and forgiving sin and rebellion. Yet he does not leave
the guilty unpunished; he punishes the children for the sin
of the parents to the third and fourth generation."

NUMBERS 14:18

*W*hy is it so hard to forgive someone? According to best-selling author and Bible teacher Joyce Meyer, "a lot of times, people feel that if they forgive the person who hurt them, then they will continue to take advantage of them and not take responsibility for what they did wrong."[25]

For several years, our production company worked as consultants for Joyce's television program, *Enjoying Everyday Life*, and got to know her personally. Off camera, she's exactly how you see her on TV—witty, intelligent, and incredibly generous. But what impressed me most was her ability to forgive people while still holding them responsible for their actions.

God has shown scripturally that He holds us responsible for our actions and will follow through with our deserved punishment. He's good, loving, slow to anger, and always merciful, which is why He has to invoke righteous punishment. Our job is to forgive those who trespass against us—completely.

■ ■ ■

Who do you need to forgive yet again? Forgive and then move on. Your health depends on it.

HEAVY LIFTING

But you, LORD are a shield around me, my glory,
the One who lifts my head high.

PSALM 3:3

*T*oday's job market is tough, especially in the business I work in—the media industry. Competition is fierce, and some estimate that it takes a minimum of ten years to achieve a breakthrough project. Even then, there's no guarantee. For creative people with delicate personalities, growing a thick skin is essential.

I've noticed that some young people naively think that God will open doors and make things happen without hard work on their part. But remember, David herded sheep and gathered rocks before he killed Goliath, and Ruth went out to the fields to gather leftover grain among strangers before she married Boaz. These biblical figures rolled up their sleeves and did the hard work. They submitted themselves to God, stayed focused, and developed useful skills.

As a child of God, we've been given talents and skills, but He expects us to develop and perfect them. Hard work matures us and brings clarity, so discipline yourself to work sacrificially—and don't forget to seek His kingdom purposes first. God will honor your heart and life. Do the heavy lifting it takes. Lift up your hands, lift up your head, and lift up Jesus. Now get to work.

■ ■ ■

What's something you're going to tackle today? Remember that God is at your side to do the heavy lifting.

Day 4

PIERCING EYES

Continue to remember those in prison as if you
were together with them in prison, and those who are
mistreated as if you yourselves were suffering.

<small>HEBREWS 13:3</small>

*T*was at a shopping mall in Dubai, United Arab Emirates, when I locked eyes with her. They were piercing. She was covered in a heavy black burka, but it was the metal cage covering her mouth that made me stare as her fashionably dressed male companion stood next to her looking at tennis shoes.

All I could do was say a silent prayer that Jesus might somehow make Himself known and bring her freedom. It was in that moment that I knew God was calling me to do something to bring His redemptive message to the women in the Middle East.

Why is it so important to reach women in the Middle East? Women are the mothers, wives, sisters, aunts, and cousins to Muslim terrorists. They are the influencers of children, and have the earliest voice in the lives of men and women who will grow up to be future freedom leaders. I've been privileged to speak and work with ministries and media groups like, SAT 7 (sat7.org), Christian Vision (cvglobal.co), and the Middle East Women's Leadership Network (mideastwomen.org), who work in many Middle Eastern countries. Each have unique ministries, but their greatest mission is to share the love and freedom of Jesus.

■ ■ ■

Women today are suffering globally. Focus on one country today and pray for the women who are trapped and need God's freedom. God hears the prayers of the righteous.

Journal

WEEK

24

HIDDEN AGENDA

Give thanks in all circumstances;
for this is God's will for you in Christ Jesus.

1 Thessalonians 5:18

I held a young boy in my arms as he sobbed. His mother, one of my closest friends, had just died the night before of cancer. We had prayed and God had miraculously brought her back to health just a few months before, but then the vicious disease with its pain and suffering returned with a fury. Why? We can never stop asking it. What is God's hidden agenda?.

The questions never end: Does God have bigger plans for us that we can't see? How can we be patient as we wait and "be anxious for nothing" (Philippians 4:6)? Can we stay open to His plans when there is real suffering taking place? And how can life's devastations bring ultimate peace?

Trusting God amidst suffering takes every bit of courage we can gather. It calls for us to stay close to His side in prayer and Bible reading. And finally, it calls for us to pull, from the depths of our soul, praise and thanksgiving for His perfect will. We may never know the reason for devastating situations or for God's agenda until we meet Him face-to-face. But we should still praise Him.

God wills for us to praise Him because when we do, He brings peace. End the *why* questions and shout *hallelujah* when suffering threatens to suffocate you. He's a breath away.

■ ■ ■

Are you suffering? What are your why questions? Praise Him while you wait. Trust Him to bring peace and hope.

Day 2

HIDE-AND-SEEK

The LORD looks down from heaven on
all mankind to see if there are any who understand,
any who seek God.

PSALM 14:2

ide-and-seek is a game that's been passed down
through the years. The game's origin is unknown, but
versions of it are played in various countries. While people hide,
the person who is "it" (the seeker) counts and then tries to find
those who are hiding. The hiders then run to the place of safety
before getting seen or tagged and thus becoming the next "it."

Like the seeker, God also pursues us. He joyously runs to
find us in our hidden places. I've often thought that when we
play this game with God, we might as well hide in a giant glass
tube because we can't hide from God. We may think we've hidden ourselves away, but our soul's guilt and shame confirms our
exposure. What we need to understand is that we're the only
ones who can break the glass tube to reach the safety of His
arms. When we hide, all we really do is keep ourselves separated from His peace and love.

In Psalm 119:32, King David, wrote, "I run in the path
of your commands, for you have broadened my understanding." Seek God and stop hiding. Instead, run in the path of His
commands.

■ ■ ■

*What's one thing you're hiding from God that is keeping you from
freedom?*

HIDING PLACE SONGS

You are my hiding place; you will protect me from
trouble and surround me with songs of deliverance.

PSALM 32:7

*S*everal years ago, I was with a film crew in a small village
outside Amsterdam. We were there to film the historic
watch shop where Corrie ten Boon and her family had con-
structed a hiding place for Jews behind a bookshelf to protect
them from being killed during World War II's Nazi occupation.
The Ten Booms were eventually caught and taken to concentra-
tion camps, and Corrie was the only one who survived to tell
the story in her book, and a later film, titled *The Hiding Place*.

We often wish for a hiding place—a secret place away from
the constant battles that can imprison our lives. Music can be a
hiding place. Songs hidden in our hearts can momentarily create
a secret respite place of God's peace in the midst of chaos. In
The Hiding Place, Corrie said she and her sister Betsie often sang
and that it is one of the reasons they were able to endure their
suffering. When discouraged, depressed, and overwhelmed, remember to sing. It will bring you hope.

■ ■ ■

*What is your favorite song of praise? Why do you love it so much?
Sing it now.*

Day 4

HIS EYE IS ON THE SPARROW

"Are not two sparrows sold for a penny? Yet not one of them
will fall to the ground outside your Father's care."

MATTHEW 10:29

My dad was a tall man for a man born in the 1920s. His mom stood around five feet tall and his dad wasn't much taller, but my dad grew up to tower over them at six feet four inches. He had to have felt out of place during his life, and this may be why he was a bit of an introvert.

Introverts are observers. After Dad's death, Mom told me she always knew Dad loved her deeply, but he found it difficult to express it verbally. I understood how she felt. I'd never doubted he loved me but seldom heard it come from his lips. As I grew into my teen years, he expressed his love to me in indirect ways, like buying me special things to eat or leaving me some extra money to go to the mall. Dad observed my needs and desires and lovingly hid money in places I'd find it. That quiet, indirect attention confirmed his constant vigilance.

Our heavenly Father also cares for us with intimate detail. He constantly provides for us, caring for our every need and desire, but often we don't notice His gifts of love. They just show up. You know, those little things, like beautiful sunsets, crashing ocean waves, and a newborn's cry. Are you paying attention to His gifts of love?

■ ■ ■

What is one intimate gift your heavenly Father has given to you? As you go about your day, keep your eyes open for his messages of love.

Journal

WEEK

25

Day 1

HOME OF THE BEAUTIFUL

And provide for those who grieve in Zion—to bestow on
them a crown of beauty instead of ashes, the oil of joy instead
of mourning, and a garment of praise instead of a spirit of
despair. They will be called oaks of righteousness, a planting
of the Lord for the display of his splendor.

ISAIAH 61:3

One of the most beautiful churches I've ever seen is located in a garbage dump in Cairo, Egypt, in a section that's inhabited by the *Zabbaleen* ("garbage collectors" in Arabic). This community of fifty thousand people recycle an estimated fifteen thousand tons (80 percent) of the city's trash yearly.[26]

The *Zabbaleen*, mostly Coptic Christians, were forced to the city outskirts by a predominately Muslim government in 1969. They worship in seven ancient churches built into rock caves, with the Monastery of Saint Simon being the largest. Each cave church is filled with awe-inspiring images of biblical figures, scenes, and scriptural references carved into the rock.[27]

Genesis 50:20 says, "You intended to harm me, but God intended it for good to accomplish what is now being done, the saving of many lives." The *Zabbaleen* are thriving and displaying God's beauty in the midst of a garbage dump. These "oaks of righteousness" have turned ashes to beauty and despair to praise, taking what was forced on them for harm and creating a display of God's splendor for the world to witness.

■ ■ ■

How has God turned ashes into beauty for you? Thank God for turning difficulty around to display His splendor.

Day 2

HOPE HAS COME

As the crowds increased, Jesus said,
"This is a wicked generation. It asks for a sign,
but none will be given it except the sign of Jonah."

LUKE 11:29

*C*rowds can quickly become overwhelming. Jesus understood this, and as crowds grew larger, He often went off
by Himself; it was His way of crowd control until the time for
His triumphal entry into Jerusalem (Matthew 18:8). Crowds
then wanted a physical sign that He was the Chosen One and the
Savior God had promised. But God had already given them one
years before—in Jonah.

Just as Jonah was called to warn the people of Nineveh to
turn from their wickedness, Jesus was called by God to do the
same. Jonah ran from God and was thrown into a dark world,
like nothing He had ever known, when he was sucked inside
the monster fish. Sequestered from the outside world, he was
tossed and tormented by the elements inside. But even there,
God heard Jonah's prayers and delivered him up to rescue God's
beloved people in Nineveh.

God did the same for us when He sent Jesus. He heard our
prayers and sent a Savior into a world where darkness prevailed.
Jesus, God's Son, came from heaven and was surrounded by the
mire of earth's sin that was destroying God's beloved creation. God
delivered a sign that is still a sign today—a Savior (Luke 2:12).

■ ■ ■

*The sign of Jonah is salvation, and our one hope is Jesus. Who will
you tell? How could you use social media to unite God's people?*

Day 3

HOPE REBELS

I consider that our present sufferings are not worth
comparing with the glory that will be revealed in us.
ROMANS 8:18

Rebellions are built on hope. Rebels choose to endure
suffering and pain for the promise of a better future.
Childbirth is similar. After nine months of preparation and
hours of labor pains, new life emerges, bringing hope for the
future.

Greeks called anxiety and devastation their future hope.
They believed that the disasters they endured were positive occurrences—change was going to be disruptive and painful, but
if change didn't happen, nothing new could break forth. Paul
had this attitude in Romans 12:12: "Be joyful in hope, patient
in affliction, faithful in prayer." He wanted us to know how to
grow our hope and see the future, and that the one and only
Hope was coming—Jesus.

When God promises something, it has already happened in
His eyes because He said it was so. We are to be patient and endure and be a Hope rebel. We can't change life's sufferings because evil has invaded this world, but God has provided for our
redemption and is preparing a new place for us (John 14:3).

■ ■ ■

*What positive occurrences in your life have come from past difficul-
ties? Remember these when you're faced with problems in the future.
Pray and endure.*

A HORRIBLE OPPORTUNITY?

For the LORD will be at your side and
will keep your foot from being snared.

PROVERBS 3:26

*T*ragedies happen. Accidents, weather-related disasters, and just crazy life occurrences. Recently, I was introduced to a talented designer in her twenties who'd been married for just a few months. She and her husband were hiking and taking pictures in some rocky canyons when he went too close to the edge and fell to his death.

Life is unpredictable, and we shake our heads and cry out to God for peace and comfort. Questions fill our minds: How can we turn horrible circumstances around and see them as opportunities for God's presence to be seen? Can we trust that God has a plan to use life's unpredictability for His purposes and kingdom? Just how do we pray when tragic things happen?

Pray that when tragedies and disasters happen, they don't snare you or send you into a tailspin. Pray that your footing be solidly placed on His promises. Surround yourself with people of hope. It's so easy to listen to how the world would react and not to the mystery of God's possibilities. Out of suffering comes joy, and out of struggles comes peace, God's way.

■ ■ ■

How do you react to the horrific things of this world? What can you do to keep your eyes fixed on God's opportunities?

Journal

WEEK

26

Day 1

I HAVE CONFIDENCE

This is the confidence we have in approaching God:
that if we ask anything according to his will, he hears us.

1 JOHN 5:14

The Sound of Music is based on the true story of a nun, Maria von Trapp, who didn't fit in. She was told to reexamine her calling and take a job as a governess for a wealthy widowed Austrian naval captain who desperately needed help with his seven children. The film is full of memorable music, but one tune that has always stood out to me is "I Have Confidence." As an actress in Hollywood for many years, I'd sing it on the way to auditions in the car. The competition for acting jobs in Hollywood is fierce and it bolstered my confidence.

John calls us to be overcomers in this Scripture. If we believe in God wholeheartedly and confidently, then obedience to His will, not ours, becomes natural. Amazingly, we always have His heart and His ears. There's nothing we desire that we can't ask of Him, but what we do need to examine is if it's the right request. Maria von Trapp prayed to be an obedient nun, and God answered her prayer by firing her as a nun, which didn't sit well with her at first. God's answers aren't always what we think they will be. God gave Maria her desire—to be obedient—and then He brought her joy unspeakable and a life she never dreamed of having.

■ ■ ■

Be confident that whatever you're asking for God hears, and He will answer according to His will. Read James 4:1–3 for extra confidence.

Day 2

HE WANTS TO PUMP YOU UP

Who shall separate us from the love of Christ?
Shall trouble or hardship or persecution or famine
or nakedness or danger or sword?

ROMANS 8:35

One of the most popular recurring skits on the TV show *Saturday Night Live* was that of Hans and Franz, two Austrian muscle jocks who promised to "pump … you up." It's a fact that as we age, we lose muscle strength and need to stay pumped up. Fitness experts tell us that along with cardio exercise, we need to do strength training for our muscles.

We also need to pump up our suffering muscle—our ability to suffer *with* Jesus. When we avoid hard situations and take the easy approach to life's issues, we depart from God's gym. We get flabby, allowing the devil to take advantage of us. Our spiritual health becomes depleted and we're unable to resist temptations. We need to work out at God's gym regularly, pump up on His Word, and do some heavy prayer lifting.

Jesus didn't flee from those who suffered or from His own suffering. He said we'd never be without troubles (John 16:33), so let's stop being wimpy weak Christians. Our nature will always choose the easy way, let's choose to build up our godly muscle with the Holy Spirit as our Trainer.

■ ■ ■

What issues do you need to work out with Jesus today? Bulk up on a new Scripture and let Jesus "pump you up."

Day 3

I'M DESPERATE FOR YOU

Listen to my cry, for I am in desperate need; rescue me from
those who pursue me, for they are too strong for me.

PSALM 142:6

Hollywood produces countless films and TV shows
about people in desperate situations. *Room* is a 2015
feature film in which Academy Award-winning actress Brie
Larson plays a woman (Joy Newsome) who was kidnapped and
had a son (Jack) during her captivity. He has never seen the
world outside the shack they've been kept in. Seven years after
her abduction, Brie is finally forced to make a life-and-death
decision that propels her in a desperate act to gain their escape.
Her plan requires her to force now five-year-old Jack to see the
reality of the grave situation they're living in.

Do you feel you're living in a grave situation? Do you feel
trapped in the life you're currently living in—captured and enslaved? Are you desperate for God's will? Or are you desperate
for a solution to your current situation and just an easy fix? God
may need to force you to see the realities of the situation you're
living in before He can help you escape them.

■ ■ ■

*What in your life has made you desperate for God? What realities do
you need to face before He can set you free? He's desperate to set you
free are you willing to let Him?*

Day 4

IN PLAIN SIGHT

He was in the world, and the world was made through him,
and the world did not know him.

JOHN 1:10

*T*he answer was staring right at me, and I couldn't see it. My brain just didn't register it. I have never been officially tested or diagnosed, but I believe I have slight learning disability.

I remember beginning my college freshmen year clueless about what I wanted to major in. But when I finally decided on elementary education and began studying about how brain malfunctions affect learning, I knew I was reading about some of the issues that had haunted me. I knew I wanted to help children who had learning issues overcome them. I graduated with a dual degree in education and special education and worked with special needs children for seven years.

I often wonder how people could have physically seen Jesus when He walked on earth and not realized who He was? His teachings, His infectious love, His miracles must have been mesmerizing. Weren't they obvious? What fear and denial a listener must have had to walk away from Him not believing after seeing Jesus in the flesh.

Jesus came from heaven to this broken world and was rejected and crucified, and today the world still doesn't see it.

■ ■ ■

What is one way you can help the world see Jesus? Ask Him to open your eyes to the things He wants to teach you that are staring right at you.

Journal

WEEK

27

OBEYING HIS VOICE AND SPURRING OTHERS ON

The LORD appeared to us in the past, saying:
"I have loved you with an everlasting love:
I have drawn you with unfailing kindness."

JEREMIAH 31:3

The 2017 film *The Shack*, based on the *New York Times* best-selling book, is a story of finding forgiveness and redemption. Mackenzie (Mack) Phillips, played by Sam Worthington, is the victim of a childhood secret that haunts him all his life. When his daughter is kidnapped and murdered, finding forgiveness for himself and from God becomes impossible. Mack returns to the shack where his daughter was killed and has a visual journey with God. Papa, played by Academy Award-winning actress Octavia Spencer, tells Mack that the reason he sees God as a woman is because he's not ready to deal with an image of God as a man.

God deals with us one issue at a time, and sometimes we're not ready to deal with the present issues until we get the past ones cleared up. The glorious thing is that God loves us with an "everlasting love" and with "unfailing kindness." He takes us at our pace.

How do we find forgiveness for ourselves and from God when horrific disasters happen? We trust in His judgment, grace, and mercy, which allows us a way to forgive and move forward.

■ ■ ■

Are you keeping a secret that only you and God know? Can you believe that God can forgive you completely? God loves you with an everlasting love. Confess it today and begin your healing.

Day 2

INEXPRESSIBLE JOY

Though you have not seen him, you love him; and even
though you do not see him now, you believe in him and
are filled with an inexpressible and glorious joy.

1 PETER 1:8

*S*everal groups of church volunteers had just returned
from feeding the poor around Kolkata, India. I could've
stretched out and taken a bath in the giant metal pots they were
cleaning. Each one could feed two hundred people, and I count-
ed ten pots. The loving volunteers had showed up at 3:00 a.m.
to cook rice and beans in the pots, which were then loaded onto
trucks and driven to various sections of the city for distribution
by 6:00 a.m.

Volunteers did this daily, and I had been given the opportunity to watch and assist at one location. The recipients patiently
stood in long lines with plastic grocery-size bags in hand, then
workers ladled the hot food into the bags while looking into
their eyes and saying, "God bless you."

As I watched the volunteers, who showed up each day to
help some of the poorest people in the world, I saw inexpressible and glorious joy. I witnessed the heart of God in action as
the volunteers made Jesus come alive in the eyes of the poor
they served. His love was evident. It was a love feast I'll never
forget.

■ ■ ■

What are some ways you could be the hands of Jesus extended to
others? Find someplace to serve the Lord so His inexpressible joy can
be seen in action.

Day 3

IS JESUS WORTH IT?

Consider it pure joy, my brothers and sisters,
whenever you face trials of many kinds, because you know
that the testing of your faith produces perseverance.

JAMES 1:2–3

*I*t's inspiring to be around Christians who have had to endure tortuous, unthinkable situations. Their devotion to God is unwavering.

A few years ago, our media production company, Cooke Pictures, filmed in Moldova, Eastern Europe, documenting the work of a ministry that rescues teenage girls. The girls had aged out of the large orphanages, where they'd spent their entire lives, and sex traffickers lay in wait for them, knowing they had no home to return to when they were released.

The following year, we were filming in Jakarta, Indonesia. We attended a church that was assisting Christians who were living in refugee camps after escaping persecution. They had come primarily from Iran, where they'd been tortured and had witnessed the death of family and friends because of their faith. I wept as I listened to their stories and heard their voices lifted to God. There was a joy in their singing and a perseverance to their lives that I'll never forget.

Both groups never complained about what they had gone through or the situations in which they found themselves. They only lifted up the name of Jesus for the joy He had brought them. Jesus was worth it to them. Is He worth it to you?

■ ■ ■

Don't miss the joy of God in the midst of your difficult circumstances. How does your life say that Jesus is worth it?

Day 4

BITTERNESS, BRAVERY, AND BREAKING DOWN WALLS

But the Jews who disbelieved stirred up the minds of the
Gentiles and embittered them against the brethren.

ACTS 14:2 NASB

It had only been a few years since the Egyptian "Arab Spring," the 2012 historic political revolution that began on social media, our world's new weapon of choice. Embittered mobs had gathered quickly, and the ministry leader who told me of the events had directly cared for wounded protesters who had been shot and sprayed with nerve gas during the revolution. He related stories of ambulances dropping victims at their doorstep, knowing the wounded protesters would be killed if they were taken to hospitals.

One of the local mosques was across the street, and the Muslim community saw the Christians taking victims in and giving them medical assistance and sanctuary. It baffled them that Christians would care for Muslims and put their own lives at risk. They crossed the street to help the Christians care for the wounded, and for many, it was the first time they had dared to speak to a Christian, whom they'd been taught to hate. Consequently, many Muslims came to believe in Christ, and the Christian church in Cairo continues to experience huge growth.

Longstanding bitterness poisons minds and twists the truths of God. Caring for the suffering breaks down walls, and some battles can only be given over to God's perfect timing.

■ ■ ■

*In what difficult situation has God helped you show love to another?
What was the outcome?*

Journal

....
....
....
....
....
....
....
....
....
....
....
....
....
....
....
....
....
....
....
....
....
....
....
....
....
....
....
....

WEEK

28

Day 1

JESUS FRUIT

"You will know them by their fruits. Grapes are not gathered
from thorn bushes nor figs from thistles, are they?"
MATTHEW 7:16 NASB

"Club Christians" are people who only show up to church
on holidays. They treat Christianity like a country club
membership—it's a social thing for them. They respect and
honor Christmas and Easter traditions but aren't serious wor-
shipers. They come up with all kinds of reasons why they can't
set time aside to actually live the life of a believer or have a
serious relationship with God. If their faith conflicts with their
lifestyle or worldview, they remain silent, unwilling to stand up
for biblical truth. Most of the time they can't defend their faith
because they know so little about it.

How do you know who the true believers and followers of
Christ are? By their fruit. You will know them by their actions.
When you truly commit to being a Christian, you regularly read
your Bible and pray so you can build a relationship with God,
you're compelled to love and care for others, and you can't hold
back sharing your faith when given an opportunity to tell others
about God's redemptive message. All three conscious choices
can result in fruit. All benefit and bring joy and hope to you,
others, and ultimately God's kingdom.

■ ■ ■

*How serious are you about your faith? Cultivate Jesus fruit. It's
deliciously rewarding.*

Day 2

JESUS STYLE

"Look, he is coming with the clouds," and "every eye will see him, even those who pierced him"; and all peoples on earth "will mourn because of him." So shall it be! Amen.

REVELATION 1:7

*Y*ouTube's most watched video to date is a music video performed by South Korean musician Psy called "Gangnam Style." This video appeared in December 2012, and to date has been viewed over 2.8 billion times, topping music charts in multiple countries.[28] His signature dance moves have even been copied by world leaders.

I choose to dance Jesus-style. Jesus created His own style, and it wasn't like anything the people of His day had seen before. He'd showed up unannounced, drew a crowd, provided food for them from almost nothing, and performed miracles. He chose to hang out with beggars, prostitutes, tax collectors, and the suffering, challenging the thinking and beliefs of those who listened. He asked questions and told stories and was known as a man of peace and love.

His life and teachings triggered one of the biggest uprisings of His time, even causing an earthquake when He was crucified. Witnesses saw and recorded His resurrection and assent to heaven.

Today, many have seen Him in dreams or in visions. His words and teachings in the Bible have yet to be proven false. But someday He'll break social media stats when "every eye will see him." He will come in the clouds, Jesus style, and we'll dance for eternity.

■ ■ ■

How has Jesus' style affected your life? How can you dance and share His style on social media?

JOIN CLUB JESUS

"If the world hates you, keep in mind that it hated me first.
If you belonged to the world, it would love you as its own.
As it is, you do not belong to the world, but I have chosen
you out of the world. That is why the world hates you."

JOHN 15:18–19

*J*oin the club! My mom would say these words to me when I lamented that it was so hard to live out my faith at times growing up.

Being a Christian today can be a challenge. Christians aren't in the hipster club, and sadly, we're often known in culture for what we're against more than what we're for. We're thought of more as the "loser club." Choosing self-restraint and living by divine direction looks radically wrong to the nonbeliever. And it often means going it alone and against the grain. The Christian club isn't a place people run to these days.

Jesus has invited you to join His club—the one where people will criticize and hate you because they hated Him. His club requires full commitment to join, but He's not asking you to go anywhere or do anything that He didn't first. Membership has benefits beyond your wildest imagination. Clarity is one. In fact, His benefits are life changing and life giving. The most important one is that Jesus owns the club and will never abandon its members or shut it down.

■ ■ ■

What benefits have you reaped from being in Club Jesus? Be a Bible-carrying member.

Day 4

YES WE CAN

For we do not have a high priest who is unable to empathize
with our weakness, but we have one who has been tempted
in every way just as we are—yet He did not sin.

HEBREWS 4:15

*F*ormer US President Barack Obama used the slogan "Yes we can" during his reelection campaign. He wanted the people of the United States to know that he couldn't lead the country alone—he needed their support. It was a brilliant political strategy and helped him win the election.

God has told us the same thing. If we want His kingdom to flourish, our effort must be united. The world doesn't see just one Christian; it sees us all lumped together. And in our present culture, it's not a favorable picture. We've failed as examples of God's freedom and joy.

Jesus exposed Himself to the same temptations we face, and set an example so we can be empathetic to others. So why aren't we? Why do we gossip and shake our heads when others have opposite lifestyles or falter in life? What's happened to God's command that we love each other as He has loved us?

When we approach unbelievers with care, humility, and forgiveness, they're given the opportunity to see Jesus and not a finger pointed in guilt and shame. It's tempting to lash out with condemnation, but God wants His people united. Yes, *we* can. *We* can care and forgive, and be peacemakers and pathways for other to see Jesus.

■ ■ ■

What can you do to change the negativity of Christianity in the world today? Spread His love and forgiveness.

Journal

WEEK

29

Day 1

JOY SHIELDS

The LORD is my strength and my shield;
my heart trusts in him, and he helps me.
My heart leaps for joy, and with my song I praise him.
PSALM 28:7

As a mom and now a grandmom, I've always loved playing music in the house. Music is essential in teaching children how to trust and obey God. Tunes we've forgotten pop up as adults, bringing renewed meaning. Proverbs 22:6 instructs us to "start children off on the way they should go, and even when they are old they will not turn from it." Many tunes are short nursery rhymes or Bible songs. The kids never seem to get tired of them, instead wanting to hear them over and over again. They've been known at times to keep me awake at night. Just like commercial jingles, the tunes get locked away in our brains, seemingly forgotten until the day they emerge anew.

When my mother passed away, the grief initially seemed overwhelming. I lay in bed, unable to do anything but sing the praise songs that came to mind. Some were silly tunes I'd memorized as a child, but their message brought a new reality. They became a shield of joy, comfort, and protection from the arrows of pain. Scriptures hidden deep in my heart also came to mind. They steadied the unstable ground, bringing peace at a time of grief. God's promises bathed me with unwavering assurances of His truths.

■ ■ ■

What are some of the praise songs and Bible verses you loved as a child? Teach them to your children so they'll have a joy shield too.

Day 2

JUMP OFF THE WALL

For the Spirit that God gave us does not make us timid,
but gives us power, love and self-discipline.

2 TIMOTHY 1:7

*W*hen I was a little girl, our house had a five-foot-tall wall built on our property line to separate the homes. I devised a way to climb up and sit on it, but the only way down was to jump. That took courage. I'd invite other kids over to play and climb the wall with me, and one of the ways I decided if I wanted to play with them again was whether they'd be brave enough to climb the wall and then jump off.

As a woman working in the media business and one who has deep faith in God, approaching tough situations like contract negotiations, employee conflicts, and financial stress is always a challenge. It requires "jumping off the wall" courage. I have to be willing to place myself into difficult and sometimes unknown situations. I have to rely on God to reveal something to me that could be an issue before I take a leap of faith.

Life is full of high walls, but God has given you a spirit of power, love, and self-discipline. You aren't alone, so take a leap of faith with Him.

■ ■ ■

What wall of fear are you sitting on today? Invite a friend over to sit on the wall with you and pray. Then jump off with the joy of Jesus.

Day 3

CROSSING OVER
TO THE LAND OF HOPE

You are about to cross the Jordan to enter and take possession
of the land the LORD is giving you. When you have taken it
over and are living there, be sure that you obey all the
decrees and laws I am setting before you today.

DEUTERONOMY 11:31–32

I knew I should have done that! How many times in my life
have I said those words? I've had countless missed opportunities that I didn't act on. Why? Procrastination, laziness,
insecurity, and an overburdened schedule are just a few of the
reasons I could name. The bottom line is that I allowed my will
to take charge and not God's.

In the Scripture verses above, God is instructing the children of Israel about the promised land they're about to enter.
He's also telling them to check their choices. The new land will
be a blessing or a curse (v. 26), depending on whether they want
to listen and obey. It's their choice.

God always leaves the decision to us. Will we obey and receive His blessings, or will we disobey and succumb to the curse
of evil, temptation, and unneeded suffering? God has given
you blessings He wants you to possess. His abundance of godly provision and wealth will allow you to flourish beyond your
wildest dreams. Cross over to His endless resources of hope.
Remember to listen up, keep Him close, and obey even when
it's difficult and doesn't make sense.

■ ■ ■

*What are you struggling with right now? Write it down so you can
name it and walkover to the land of Hope.*

Day 4

GENEROSITY CATALYST

> "But store up for yourselves treasures in heaven,
> where moths and vermin do not destroy,
> and where thieves do not break in and steal."
>
> MATTHEW 6:20

David Green, founder of Hobby Lobby, said in his book *Giving It All Away … and Getting It All Back Again*, "We are put on this earth to give, to devote ourselves to a radical brand of generosity that changes lives and leaves a legacy. Generosity begins with an attitude that extends into every aspect of life, not just money."[29] David is one of the most generous men I've ever met, and his example has taught his children and now his grand-children the importance of radical giving. He's living a legacy that will be here long after God takes him to heaven, and knows that living on earth is temporary and that eternity is what matters. It is where our treasure should be.

How do we create heavenly treasure while we're on earth? We radically give, but not just our money. We give our time and our love, and extend mercy even when wronged. We become generous givers and boldly battle selfishness with a world-changing force. We do it loudly, quietly, boldly, sacrificially, and endlessly. When we do, we leave an unforgettable legacy.

■ ■ ■

How could you be a radical giver? Look for new ways to boldly trust God and become a catalyst for generosity.

Journal

WEEK

30

Day 1

GOD'S TREASURED PEOPLE

"On that day no one who is on the housetop, with possessions inside, should go down to get them. Likewise, no one in the field should go back for anything. Remember Lot's wife!"

LUKE 17:31–32

*G*lobally, we're witnessing what might be the largest migration of refugees that's ever occurred in history. Sixty million people, or 1 in 100 (1 in 20 in the Middle East and 1 in 60 in continental Africa), have been forcibly displaced according to Pew research, as of 2016.[30] Aleppo, the capital of and once the largest city in Syria, is now a pile of rubble. It's estimated by Reuters (as of December 2016) that 30,000 people have been evacuated from that city alone.[31] Families have been split apart and killed. So what does this mean to us?

Refugees are family too. We're related by the blood of Jesus. Jesus showed us, in Matthew 12:48–50, that our earthly family, the one we've been born into, is not our only family. We also have a global family that we become a part of when we unite with our heavenly Father. In Luke 18:22, Jesus told the rich man to "sell everything" and he'd have "treasure in heaven." It's people that matter to God; people are His treasures, and there are many who are suffering today. Will you help the people God loves as much as you ?

■ ■ ■

What are your doing for the global family of God? The refugees in our world are many, and some are your Christian brothers and sisters. Get involved.

LIVID AND LOVED

Jesus answered: "Watch out that no one deceives you.
For many will come in my name, claiming,
'I am the Messiah,' and will deceive many."

MATTHEW 24:4–5

*S*he was *livid*. All her life she'd been abused and made to live in shame. She was a new Christian in Iraq, having converted from Islam, and had learned that Moses brought the law, not Mohammad. Then she learned that Jesus had brought further freedom from those ancient laws when, as the Son of God, He came to earth and gave His life as a sacrifice for her sin and shame. Jesus had redeemed her. He'd paid the price for her shame—shame that had kept her in bondage. But she was most infuriated about how Mohammad had deceived entire nations and had put them back under his law. She was fiery mad but knew her only hope was to forgive. Forgive and love as Jesus, her newfound Father, had done and was teaching her to do.

Jesus came to set us free (Matthew 8:32). This former women's leader of the Islamic faith was living in a completely new world. Not one without problems and horrific pain and suffering, but one in which she could live triumphantly regardless. Her family had been killed and her home bombed. They had died not knowing the truth of Jesus and had only known the lies of Mohammad, and she wept.

■ ■ ■

How fully have you grasped the freedom of redemptive grace? Has the truth set your free? "You … [are] free indeed" (John 8:36).

Day 3

AGENDAS AND SCHEDULES

Therefore we do not lose heart. Though outwardly we are
wasting away, yet inwardly we are being renewed day by day.
For our light and momentary troubles are achieving for
us an eternal glory that far outweighs them all.

2 CORINTHIANS 4:16—17

My husband is an "early bird," but I tend to be more
of a "night owl." At what time of day do you focus
and do your best work? Are you locked into someone else's
schedule, allowing their agendas to run yours? Are you punch-
ing a time clock that's keeping you from being creative and all
that God wants you to be? Whose agenda is more important,
yours or Gods? We all have different responsibilities and ways of
working, but is there a way to work and live a lifestyle we can
actually thrive in? The one God wants for us?

We get depressed when we lock ourselves into schedules and
obligations of our own choosing, not considering God's agenda.
Momentary pressures and struggles will come, but we can choose
to live above them and to follow His plan. Often we use time as an
excuse: "I don't have time to go back to school"; "I don't have time
to go to that conference"; "I don't have time to …"

Time is not an excuse in the kingdom of God. Yes, we're all
getting older, but God renews us inwardly each day if we connect with Him and allow His plans and timetable to proceed.
God's schedule is always perfect.

■ ■ ■

*What excuses are you using for poor planning or an inability to
make hard choices? Examine your time today and let God renew you
inwardly.*

LOVE LANGUAGE

> If I speak in the tongues of men or of angels, but do not
> have love, I am only a resounding gong or a clanging cymbal.
>
> 1 CORINTHIANS 13:1

I sat in a prayer circle of influential women who had come from all over the globe for a special gathering. We shed tears as our hearts opened to God's presence and we shared our prayer requests. The wife of a leading Ukrainian official began to pray. She spoke very little English, so none of us knew a word of what she was saying, but our hearts did. The love of God in her heart, and our united hearts together, translated her words and message.

The language of God's love is always understood. Our minds may fail in translating, but our hearts never do. It's mysterious and awe inspiring how God brings understanding. There are no language barriers with Him. Amid our constant efforts to connect and break down walls that keep us separated, God wants us to remember that love has a language all its own. And it's powerful. With all our ambitious "do good" work for others, if we lack love, ears remain deaf. The embrace of love is the only language that unifies, translates, and breaks through.

■ ■ ■

What language are you using? The world listens when God's love language is spoken. Be sure you're not a "clanging cymbal."

Journal

WEEK

34

Day 1

LYIN' EYES

Then Judas Iscariot, one of the Twelve, went to the
chief priests to betray Jesus to them. They were delighted
to hear this and promised to give him money.
So he watched for an opportunity to hand him over.

MARK 14:10–11

The 1975 Eagles hit song "Lyin' Eyes" was written by Glenn
Frey and Don Henley. The inspiration for the song sup-
posedly came when they were eating dinner at a popular Beverly
Hills restaurant that was frequented by wealthy men and beautiful young women who were cheating on their husbands and
wives. The final verse of the song reflects our inability to change
without God's intervention. We can't stop our selfish desires
and our lyin' eyes.

The song tells about how we like to "arrange" things and that
we never change even when we find a new lover or something
better. Without God's intervention, our nature looks for opportunities to "arrange" desires. Judas had spent almost three years
with Jesus as a close companion. He was one of the twelve disciples and knew Jesus intimately, yet this didn't change things for
him. In the end, he allowed his old nature and desires to over-
take what he knew was wrong. "The night he betrayed Jesus,
[Judas] said, 'Surely you don't mean me, Rabbi?' Jesus answered
him, 'You have said so'" (Matthew 26:25). Judas' lyin' eyes betrayed him.

■ ■ ■

*What's in your past nature? Keep your desires in check. God sees how
you arrange things.*

Day 2

MANGROVES

But he was pierced for our transgressions, he was crushed
for our iniquities; the punishment that brought us peace
was on him, and by his wounds we are healed.

ISAIAH 53:5

*O*n a trip to Costa Rica, I took a boat up the river to observe the plant and wildlife surrounding the rainforest.
Mangrove trees grow along the banks of the rivers that lead
out to the oceans, thriving in saltwater even though plants need
fresh water to grow. These trees are essential in filtering the water, and I wondered how they got rid of the salt they consumed.
Our guide told us that they filter out some of the salt through
their roots and into "sacrificial" leaves that turn yellow and die,
sacrificing themselves so the tree can live.

Nature reflects the story of God's love to us. God sent His
Son to sacrificially die for us so we might live. Jesus took on our
sins and died so we could survive and even thrive. We are then
to be salt in the world (Matthew 5:13). If we're to be useful
to God, we must ourselves become salty leaves, which sometimes even requires us to give up our lives. The glorious magnif-
icence of God's grace is that we've been healed by the sacrifice
of Jesus. If we lose our life for Him, we'll find it. God said this
three times in Scripture (Matthew 10:39; 16:25; Mark 8:35).
Remember His promise and let it bring you undying hope.

■ ■ ■

*Do you want your life to grow and thrive? Lose your old one. How
can you become salty and sacrificial?*

Day 3

ME AND MY SHADOW

He who dwells in the shelter of the Most High
will rest in the shadow of the Almighty.

PSALM 91:1

The 1927 song "Me and My Shadow," written by Billy Rose and recorded by some of the top recording artists of all time, captures the world's loneliness. Depression is an unwelcome companion that seems ever present in our lives. It shadows us down every avenue of our lives.

In our challenging world with endless suffering, it's inevitable that depression and loneliness will haunt us. The Bible says satan prowls the earth, "looking for someone to devour" (1 Peter 5:8). He shadows us and loves to upend our lives with emotions that bring us to our knees.

But when we stay inside God's shelter, depression and loneliness vanish. God created our souls to be with Him so we'd have a place of peace. When we seek the worthless trinkets the world dangles in front of our eyes, hoping to find contentment, we invite emptiness and depression.

God wants us to "dwell" not on momentary happiness but on His eternal joy. The next time you start feeling blue, choose to trust God and walk down His avenue of joy. God's always there and He'll keep you tap-dancing.

■ ■ ■

What other Scriptures have you memorized to dispel loneliness? Keep finding new ones. Share these with others when they're blue.

Day 4

REFUGE WHEN
THE EARTH QUAKES

I will say to the Lord, "He is my refuge and my fortress,
my God, in whom I trust."

PSALM 91:1–2

My French grandmother and her sisters came to America in 1906, just a few weeks before the famed San Francisco earthquake. The seismic event leveled the city, including the mansion where she was living and working as a maid. The earthquake still holds the record as the largest loss of life by any earthquake in California history. I never fully understood Mimi's courage until I moved to California, where I too have been awakened in in the middle of the night by a terrifying earthquake. I have deep admiration for her courage and tenacity as a young woman.

We live in uncertain times. There are thousands of homeless people on streets every night in America and we are seeing countless numbers of Middle East and Northern African immigrants escaping their countries and looking for refuge due to war and persecution.

A brick-and-mortar safe dwelling place may not always be guaranteed in life, but God has promised that in Him we will always have a spiritually secure place for our souls no matter where we're forced to lay our heads at night. When the earth shakes, find rest in God's arms. He is your refuge and fortress.

■ ■ ■

What is God calling you to do for those who need refuge where you live? Take that step and be God's fortress extended on earth.

Journal

WEEK

33

Day 1

NONCOMPETITIVE
AND COMPLIMENTARY

In your relationships with one another, have the same
mindset as Christ Jesus: Who, being in very nature God,
did not consider equality with God something to be used to
his own advantage; rather, he made himself nothing by taking
on the very nature of a servant, being made in human likeness.

PHILIPPIANS 2:5–7

I'm my husband's better half. Many times, I've said these
words to audiences to get a laugh. That said, it's not true.
What's made our marriage flourish is that I'm not his *better* half;
I'm his *complimentary* half.

Most of us never seem to stop competing with each other.
Our world cultivates this attitude, and the feminist movement
will never call a truce. Jesus set an example for us when He
never considered being His Father's equal. He sought nothing
for Himself, instead choosing to do God's will.

God has laid out in several places in Scripture how He wants
us to function as men and women. He instructs us to submit to
Him first and then to respect and honor each other, laying down
our lives for each other. It requires that we change cultural mind-
sets and think differently. When we take on the mind of Christ,
we humble ourselves as He did by leading with graciousness.

When male and female competition ends, eternal things
are accomplished and unity and love flourishes. Read Ephesians
5:24–27 and become a proponent of getting it right.

■ ■ ■

*Open a door, offer a seat, step aside. What can you do today for
people of the opposite sex to honor them and set an example of God's
attitude of gracious gender equality?*

195

MOM'S ABUNDANT LIFE

"The thief comes only to steal and kill and destroy;
I have come that they may have life, and have it abundantly."

JOHN 10:10

*I*t must have been well over one hundred degrees in the Nevada desert that day in August 1960. My family's banana-yellow station wagon lurched and sputtered as the engine failed, and my dad guided it to the side of the road. We were miles from the next gas station. Dad soon hitched a ride with a passing truck, leaving me and my two older brothers in my mother's care. My older brother, Richard, got out of the car and immediately threw rocks as Robbie, a miracle baby, gasped for breath in the back seat. Born with a missing heart valve, he underwent experimental surgery. A team of surgeons replaced this vital part with a pig's valve, hoping he would live. The heat of the day was making it difficult for him to breathe.

What seemed like hours began to wear on my fearful five-year-old patience and I started to cry. Mom had to have been worried too, but she didn't show it. Her peace that day is something I'll never forget, as she held me close and said, "Kathy, God's taken us this far. He's going to take us all the way home." Her faith was undaunting.

Life can hold unfathomable challenges, but God hasn't lost sight of us. He's with us on what seems like abandoned desert roads or hospital rooms. He'll continue to be there to take us all the way home.

■ ■ ■

What is one thing you fear? How can God's peace and provision comfort you today?

Day 3

PARENTAL INSTINCT

When the wine was gone, Jesus' mother said to him,
"They have no more wine." "Woman, why do you
involve me?" Jesus replied. "My hour has not yet come."

JOHN 2:3–4

When my oldest daughter, Kelsey, at four years of age, stole the solo presentation at the Christmas show, I instantly knew she was going to be a performer. And she hasn't proven me wrong. Today she's what we call in the business "a triple threat"—an actor, singer, and dancer.

Mary, the mother of Jesus, also used her motherly instinct at the wedding where Jesus turned water to wine. I've often wondered if she wasn't a guest, but the wedding planner. Was she responsible for the wine and serving it? Jesus was there as a guest, and it wasn't his concern when the wine was gone, hence his comment in our Scripture today. Mary needed help and she knew where to get it; her instinct told her that her son could do miracles.

Parents need to help their children realize what their talents and skills are encouraging and assisting them in becoming what God's called them to be. Mary felt Jesus' hour had come and it was time for Him to perform a miracle and fulfill His earthly mission. God commanded children to obey their parents, and Jesus realized He needed to obey His mom.

■ ■ ■

If you're a parent, what talents and skills are you seeing in your children? Pray that God will give you insight into how you can help them grow into who He's called them to be.

Day 4

MASTERING LIFE

"No one can serve two masters. Either you will hate the one
and love the other, or you will be devoted to the one and
despise the other. You cannot serve both God and money."

MATTHEW 6:24

*H*ave you looked at your checkbook and your calendar lately? When you look closely, notice how you spend your money and time. It will tell you what really matters in your life. Are you enslaved to wrong choices? Who or what's mastering your life?

Jesus couldn't have said it any clearer: Either we'll follow the world's agenda and let it master us or we'll pick God's agenda. We can't do both, and it centers on fear. Are you afraid if you don't show up for an event or stay late at your job that you won't get ahead or you'll lose your competitive edge? Do you take on more work because you've overspent on luxuries and you're afraid you won't be able to pay your bills? Is your desire for money controlling your time, and do you spend more time on temporary distractions while longing for lasting contentment that only God can bring? Jesus said how you want to live is your choice, but only one choice is possible—either the world's way or His way.

■ ■ ■

What answers did you give to the questions above? If you don't like them, create an alternative plan. Then find ways to teach your children and grandchildren how to choose the right master for their lives.

Journal

WEEK

33

Day 1

MORE THAN ENOUGH

So all the skilled workers who were doing all the work
on the sanctuary left what they were doing and said to Moses,
"The people are bringing more than enough for doing
the work the LORD commanded to be done."

EXODUS 36:4–5

At a leadership gathering of ministers from around the world, I was inspired by hearing how God's hand of provision was flourishing in many chaotic, destructive war zones. There is still much need, but the church is flourishing because God's people are willing to give sacrificially.

When God commanded Moses to build the tabernacle and construct altar pieces and elements for worship inside it, Moses went to the people. He couldn't do it alone. It took teams of talented and skilled workers whom God had prepared, along with the willing hearts of those who had learned the importance of giving. What's interesting about this Scripture is that the people trusted God and Moses so completely that they gave more than what was required. In fact, the leaders had to stop working to come tell Moses to instruct the people to stop giving. What a welcome problem that must have been.

When a community of God's people unites, His abundance fills the temple, and there is more than enough. He's glorified and amazing things get accomplished.

■ ■ ■

Was there a time when you gave sacrificially so the body of Christ could flourish? What could you share today out of the talents, skills, and abundance God has given you?

WEALTH UNTOLD

> "Do not store up for yourselves treasures on earth,
> where moths and vermin destroy,
> and where thieves break in and steal."
>
> MATTHEW 6:19

*F*or a fleeting moment, I felt ashamed. I had returned home to attend my ten-year high school reunion and hadn't seen most of my classmates for years. I walked confidently into the hotel ballroom, and Steve, the class president, was the first person who spoke to me. We'd gone through school together from kindergarten, and what came out of his mouth (I think) was meant to be a compliment: "You sure look different from that first day of kindergarten. I remember you had holes in your pants that day."

The comment hit hard. It brought back memories of my brother's death and my family's financial hardships during that time. For a moment, I was embarrassed I wasn't born into wealth. Until, in my next breath, I realized I *had* been. God revealed to me I had been given greater wealth. I had the knowledge of who I was in Jesus—a member of His royal family. Through the challenges of my childhood, He taught me to trust Him and to seek treasure not from earth's coffers but from His eternal wisdom. In an instant, I saw the value of building a relationship with God that no one can take away or destroy. He has wealth untold for you. Do you trust Him?

■ ■ ■

Where does your true treasure lie? Write down the most important things in your life, then ask God what needs to change.

Day 3

MY ONLY HOPE

Then Asa called to the LORD his God and said, "LORD, there
is no one like you to help the powerless against the mighty.
Help us, LORD our God, for we rely on you, and in your
name we have come against this vast army. LORD, you are
our God; do not let mere mortals prevail against you."

2 CHRONICLES 14:11

"*T*his is our most desperate hour. Help me, Obi-Wan Kenobi.
You're my only hope." That's the message Princess Leia
programed into R2-D2 in *Star Wars: Episode IV—A New Hope*.[32]
The first time I saw the film, my husband and I had just been
married and he was a budding director. When it ended, I turned
to him and said, "Let's watch it again. Now!" Great stories make
you want to experience them repeatedly.

We've all been in desperate situations and in need of hope.
In our Scripture today, Asa needed to reach his Supreme
Commander. He cried out to God, our one true Hope.
Sometimes in life, we may feel as if we're just uploading a dis-
tress message into a robot, but God has promised to hear our
cries and deliver us from trouble (Psalm 34:17).

Asa told God to "not let mere mortals prevail"; he recognized God's supremacy. Do you? God's not in a galaxy far, far
away. Don't let your mortality stop your deliverance.

■ ■ ■

*What desperate situation are you in right now? Remember that God
isn't science fiction. He's real and you can depend on Him for all
your voyages.*

Day 4

NO ORPHANS
IN GOD'S KINGDOM

For I am convinced that neither death nor life, neither angels nor
demons, neither the present nor the future, nor any powers, neither
height nor depth, nor anything else in all creation, will be able to
separate us from the love of God that is in Christ Jesus our Lord.

ROMANS 8:38–39

It felt like a scene from the Charles Dickens book *Oliver Twist* as I sat with a group of three- and four-year-olds in an orphanage in Eastern Europe. It was a bitter-cold day, and the orphanage felt more like a bleak prison camp with its encasing high stone walls. Timid children lined up for their daily bowl of mush, a serving of cucumbers and tomatoes, and a glass of milk.

My heart broke knowing that the beautiful children I'd been hugging and holding that morning might one day be victims of sex crimes, which had been the fate of many who had come from there.

The young ministry leaders I was with that day had grown up and been rescued by Christians but returned regularly to bring God's message of hope to the love starved children abandoned there. They had been shown the healing and restoring power of an eternal heavenly Father—one who would never abandon them. Nothing can ever separate them from His love, and now they were committed to bringing hope to those young children who needed it so desperately.

■ ■ ■

*Do you know someone who has been abandoned and has lost hope?
Become the light of hope and tell them about God's love. There are
no orphans in God's kingdom.*

204

Journal

Day 1

PERFECT TIMING

Overhearing what they said, Jesus told him,
"Don't be afraid; just believe."

MARK 5:36

*I*n Lewis Carroll's classic children's story *Alice's Adventures in Wonderland*, the White Rabbit is always late, running so behind that he doesn't even have the time to say hello or good-bye. Many days, I think I've met this White Rabbit. He's me, as I'm always running from one thing to the next in a whirlwind. I know my husband often feels like Alice—always perplexed and a bit perturbed with me.

Jesus was never perplexed or perturbed by the suffering crowds. When Jairus asked Him to come quickly because his daughter was dying, Jesus didn't hesitate but was quickly overwhelmed by crowds who also were desperate for God's healing. He didn't fret over His tardiness even though Jairus lost hope when he learned his daughter had died. Jesus just kept going. And at His perfect pace, He comforted Jairus with these words: "Don't be afraid; just believe."

And like the Master of heaven and of earth that He is still today, God continues to work at His pace and heals according to His timing and not ours. Don't ever lose hope. There are no rabbit trails with God. And He's never wrong or late.

■ ■ ■

Are you perplexed with what seems like God's tardiness? Confess your unbelief and "be not afraid." God's never late. He'll bring comfort and answers in His perfect time.

NOT AGAIN!

Let perseverance finish its work so that you
may be mature and complete, not lacking anything.

JAMES 1:4

*D*o *I have to practice again?* I remember those words regularly coming out of my young daughter's mouth every day when we sat down for piano practice. "I wish I'd been born in another family," Bailey would say. "None of my friends have to practice."

My reply was always, "Sorry, you're part of this family, not your friends'." Her immaturity kept her from seeing the talent I saw as a parent; she lacked the perseverance to see how learning to play would someday be a blessing and benefit. Now as an adult, she prays for the day when she can quit her "day job" to spend all her time on writing music and performing.

God has given you talents and has plans for you that may be hidden because of your immaturity. Are you willing to persevere and labor for the rewards and plans He has in store for you? Learning a skill or honing a talent can feel laborious. It can be a lonely road when none of your friends are doing the same thing, but God is disciplining you, so persevere. He wants you to have that abundant life that's perfectly fulfilling and lacking nothing. One filled with beautiful music.

■ ■ ■

*Are there talents God's given you that you haven't come to fruition?
How will you change that today?*

NOTHING'S NEW

What has been will be again, what has been done
will be done again; there is nothing new under the sun.

ECCLESIASTES 1:9

*W*atching my daughter give birth and seeing new life emerge was unforgettable. I vividly remembered giving birth to her and how much physical work it had been. But the laboring to bring forth life is one of the greatest joys a woman can ever experience. It's immediately followed by the laborious task of raising them. "Children are a heritage from the LORD" (Psalm 127:3).

Solomon is considered by biblical historians to be the wisest man in the world, and he knew that God would one day bring everything into His final judgment, but that until then, we will labor "under the sun" (Ecclesiastes 1:3; 2:8) and then die. It can be depressing to think about unless you know what's worthwhile. Solomon's conclusion is that in all our striving, all that really matters is that we fear God and obey Him (12:13–14).

We are doomed to labor at something all our lives until we labor for our last breath. Learn from a wise man. Labor for the kind of love, hope, and joy that only God can bring. Labor to know, fear, and obey God, and in doing so your labors will not be in vain.

■ ■ ■

Do you want to gain wisdom and clarity? Think about how you can labor not for riches but to know God more. How do you think that might change your life's perspective?

Day 4

ONE BIG THING

Brothers and sisters, I do not consider myself yet to
have taken hold of it. But one thing I do: Forgetting what
is behind and straining toward what is ahead.

PHILIPPIANS 3:13

I was a pom-pom-carrying cheerleader from age four until the end of college. With a basketball coach for a dad, I was immersed in the game and loved to cheer on teams. On a deeper level, that's who I am at my core.

My husband, Phil Cooke, wrote a book titled *One Big Thing: Discovering What You Were Born to Do* to answer the burning question of purpose. We're all passionate about things in life, but we each have one thing God has called us to do. He designed each of us with unique talents and gifts (which is Phil's other book, *Unique: Telling Your Story in the Age of Brands and Social Media*), but they're just tools for us. Discovering who we are at our core is key in using those tools to fulfill what God's called us to do—our purpose.

Is it time for you to move past what you thought you were supposed to do, and start becoming what God's called you to be? I'm still a cheerleader, rooting for family and friends, but what I'm constantly striving to be is a better cheerleader for my Savior, Jesus Christ. I'm made to champion those around me, but I've failed if my talents and abilities don't glorify Him first.

■ ■ ■

Who are you cheering for in life? What's the one big thing God has created you to be?

Journal

Day 1

EASY TO SHARE,
HARDER TO RECEIVE

*He received honor and glory from God the Father when
the voice came to him from the Majestic Glory, saying,
"This is my Son, whom I love; with him I am well pleased."*

2 PETER 1:17

"No! Me no want to share," my three-year-old granddaughter wailed. To which her mother immediately said the dreaded word, "Time-out!" Off she was sent to the hallway chair she knew so well.

It's hard for children to learn to share. But what may be even more difficult as adults is learning how to receive and allowing others to bless us with gifts of love. Receiving puts us in a vulnerable position of admitting we lack something and aren't enough.

We can also be stubborn about receiving God's spiritual gifts. Jesus was just starting His ministry, but first He wanted to mentor us in how to die to self so we can receive. Jesus submitted himself to the Father by the act of water emersion. This act is a sign of dying and rising again, to live in submission to God. What came next is often missed. Jesus received. He allowed Himself to be blessed by God—honored and praised. Are you beating yourself up because of imperfections and inabilities to live perfectly and sinless? Jesus took care of that on the cross. Live fully in God's ever-redeeming grace. You are a child of God, who yes, still gets sent to the "time-out chair" but is loved with an everlasting love.

■ ■ ■

God is proud of you. Take that in for a few minutes. How does it feel?

Day 2

PAINT A FEARLESS PICTURE

Not that we are competent in ourselves to claim anything for
ourselves, but our competence comes from God.

2 CORINTHIANS 3:5

*I*n my experience, insecurity and fear keep people from achieving greatness more than anything else in life. While at an event in Washington, DC, I was invited to participate in a painting class. I was a bit hesitant, if not intimidated. Even though I consider myself a creative person, the thought of being exposed as an inept painter was petrifying. Nevertheless, I forced myself to go. We held up our paintings for a group picture at the end of the class, and the paintings were diverse yet beautiful. No two were alike.

When we step into fear, we step away from the safety nets we've built around ourselves. We rob ourselves of freedom and joy by staying in safe places. God wants to bring us into unfamiliar environments that will deepen our dependence on Him to overcome new challenges.

I'm not ready to quit my day job to become a painter, but God gave me a new perspective on how to step into the unknown and trust the abilities He's given me. He uses the beauty of our individuality to accomplish His unique purposes if we're fearless.

■ ■ ■

What talent have you hidden away because of fear of exposure? Try doing something you've always wanted to do today but were afraid to attempt.

■ ■

Day 3

PEOPLE OF WALMART

He grew up before him like a tender shoot, and like a root
out of dry ground. He had no beauty or majesty to attract us
to him, nothing in his appearance that we should desire him.

ISAIAH 53:2

There is a popular website called People of Walmart (peopleofwalmart.com). A warning, the pictures can be astonishing, but many of them are also hilarious. The pictures portray people who show up in all kinds of clothes (or lack of them) and are all kinds of sizes and shapes, on a quest to find a shopping bargain. It's a vivid reminder that God has made each of us unique.

I wonder, if Jesus walked the earth today, would we find Him shopping at Walmart? When He was on the earth, He went where the people were and confronted them in their environments. He didn't let race, gender, financial status, physical ability, or personality deter Him—and He particularly searched out those who were shunned by society or considered odd.

When I consider the diversity of the people on this website, frankly I don't understand some of them. But I thank God that He gives me compassion for those I'd be hesitant to hang out or go shopping with. Christ who lives in me allows me to see them how He sees them. He's wholeheartedly inclusive, and we need to be too.

■ ■ ■

What types of people do you mistrust on sight alone? Enter into Jesus' inclusive love. His arms are outstretched to all, even the people of Walmart.

PIN IT

Let us not become weary in doing good. For at the
proper time we will reap a harvest if we do not give up.

GALATIANS 6:9

*T*he popular social media site Pinterest gives us lots of ideas, allowing us to "pin" our likes together to focus and sort them.

Our homes and office environments are full of personal items and collections that are generally worthless. But to us they're priceless. I have an old plaster plaque from 1950 that belonged to my mother. It hung in our house in a prominent place growing up, and now it hangs in my office, proclaiming, *Jesus Never Fails*. I cherish it because of its truth and because Mom found Jesus to be unfailing all her life.

Over the years, I watched my mother do a lot of good. She was a loving wife and mother, volunteered at church, and was successful in real estate. She also experienced lots of doors slamming in her face because people didn't understand her passion of wanting them to know Jesus. But she persevered, helping many people through their suffering, and I thank God there are many people who will call heaven their home because of Mom's determination in letting them know that Jesus never fails.

■ ■ ■

What will you "pin" today that will leave a lasting example of faith for your family and friends? What do you want them to remember?

Journal

WEEK

36

TINY LIGHTS

> "Believe in the light while you have the light,
> so that you may become children of light."
>
> JOHN 12:36

*H*omes today are full of electronic devices and appliances with tiny lights that indicate if they are on or off. These pesky devices fill my room at night and keep me awake.

We all know that light is needed to see, which is why Jesus gave us this association in the verse above. His light brings great truth, but to those who don't understand or who don't know Him, it's pesky. It's irritating because it exposes our godlessness. Born into a dark world, we eventually come to the knowledge of good and evil, and the spiritual part of us has to be addressed. Our mind asks, *Is there a God?* We can't turn off the pin light.

Christians often feel they have to turn on floodlights to expose God's light to nonbelievers. But in today's culture, pin lights are all that people need to begin to see Jesus. God's pin light is on in each of us. Let's be careful not to send nonbelievers running for protection because we've laser-tagged them or are irritatingly pesky.

■ ■ ■

Are you that intimate light or are you overexposing Jesus' light? What can you do to turn up or turn down the glow?

THE FAITH OF MARTIN LUTHER

For in the gospel the righteousness of God is revealed—
a righteousness that is by faith from first to last,
just as it is written: "The righteous will live by faith."

ROMANS 1:17

This verse was reportedly one of Martin Luther's favorite Scriptures. An iconic Christian theologian still today, Luther was the first person to translate the Greek New Testament into German. He believed that by faith—our belief and trust in Jesus—and not by the things we do, God redeems us for eternity. The year 2017 is the 500th anniversary of the Protestant Reformation. In 1517, Luther helped instigate the Reformation by nailing his Ninety-Five Theses for the reform of the Catholic Church on the doors of Castle Church in Wittenberg, Germany.

Several years ago, just after the Berlin Wall fell, and again in 2017 while shooting a film, I was able to visit Wittenberg and reflect on this great man of faith. Luther was a real guy. He was an admitted sinner, short tempered, and opinionated, and was known to have had stomach issues requiring considerable amounts of time on the toilet. Maybe that's the reason he called the Catholic pope at that time a fart. But Luther was passionate, right down to his love for beer and his devotion to his wife, Katharine von Bora. Although his writings are not perfect, his unwavering faith and thoughts are worth our reflection.

■ ■ ■

What truths has God taught you? Do you have a few favorite Bible verses? Write down three of them today and spend some time reflecting on how they've affected your life.

■ ■

Day 3

POP YOUR BUBBLE

Do not deceive yourselves. If any of you think you
are wise by the standards of this age, you should
become "fools" so that you may become wise.

<small>1 Corinthians 3:18</small>

*H*ave you ever heard the saying "Don't be so heavenly
minded that you're no earthly good"?

We may be doing lots of good, but by *not* stepping outside of
the church crowd occasionally, we can become partially sighted
and can even cause harm. As I travel the world, I'm increasingly
aware that good leadership comes from listening and not just
acquiring information.

Wisdom comes from understanding culture, history, and
diversity. We should never compromise biblical truths, but we
can't negate or belittle the perspectives of those who have opposite worldviews. To walk in wisdom we need to be able to
speak the language of the culture and debate contemporary issues intelligently. If we isolate ourselves, we risk becoming nar-
row minded and losing our effectiveness as representatives of
God's kingdom. If we're irrelevant—if people disregard us—
we're no heavenly good.

Jesus respected people, even the ones society shunned. And
He went into controversial places and engaged difficult issues. By
knowing how people thought, He changed their mind-set. His final words on the cross, "Father, forgive them, for they do not know
what they are doing" (Luke 23:34), are an example of His compassionate and accepting heart right up to the end.

■ ■ ■

*How could you participate in the lives of people who may think dif-
ferently from you? Always start with compassion.*

Day 4

POUNDING THE PAVEMENT

> For you know that you ought to imitate us. We were not
> idle when we were with you. We never accepted food from
> anyone without paying for it. We worked hard day and night
> so we would not be a burden to any of you.
>
> 2 Thessalonians 3:7–8 NLT

Thousands of people flood Hollywood weekly seeking stardom. Sadly, few succeed. As in all areas of life, success in the entertainment and media industry comes from hard work. People must be willing to do the foundational pounding of the pavement until a breakthrough takes place, which can take years.

God blesses us with skills and talents, and He expects us to use them as tools to accomplish His kingdom purposes first. Each day is an opportunity given to do something, meet someone, or learn something that can influence another for the kingdom of God. We need to pay attention to His will first and then look for opportunities for our personal success. God works in mysterious ways. Opportunities come suddenly and from unexpected places.

He is at our side, mentoring us with His Word and in our moment-to-moment daily communication with Him. Success is where talent and hard work merge before that swinging open door of opportunity slams shut. When we seek Him, God clears our eyes to see those doors that swing wide open.

■ ■ ■

How can He help you pound the pavement for your success? Work diligently for Him and look for His doors of opportunity.

Journal

WEEK

37

DEFYING GRAVITY

So the sun stood still, and the moon stopped. ...
The sun stopped in the middle of the sky and delayed
going down about a full day.

JOSHUA 10:13

*H*ow could the sun possibly stand still? It would be like defying gravity. That's why scientists, mathematicians, and storytellers have tried to explain, prove, or disprove this biblical occurrence as documented in Joshua.

Hollywood can make anything that's fake look real. My challenge to those who believe in God and in what's written in the Bible is that we don't twist or inflate His truth to make God look fake. When we accept Christ, He transforms us. No, we don't become some alien that transforms into a machine, but something does happen to our hearts that affects our minds and changes our thinking. Our previous life choices suddenly aren't as attractive. We begin to want to make godly choices. New Christians are sometimes called "fake" or told to "get real" because God can so radically transform their lives that they become vastly different. Even their appearance changes. For individuals who have been strung out on substance abuse or have suffered with huge emotional challenges, Christ's transformation is a miracle. It defies gravity.

I've seen unexplainable miracles that defy science and the laws of nature, and I believe we're going to see more. Jesus told us in John 14:12 that we'd do "even greater things" than the works He did while on the earth.

■ ■ ■

What miracles has God done in your life? In what ways have they been sun-stopping or gravity-defying miracles?

Day 2

HANDS UP

Therefore I want the men everywhere to pray,
lifting up holy hands without anger or disputing.

1 TIMOTHY 2:8

*I*n Los Angeles, regular TV programing is often interrupted by breaking news about police car chases. Once the suspects finally stop, they must raise their hands, back out of the car, and lie face down on the pavement. Without complete surrender, the police won't move in.

Walking into many Christian churches today, observers will see participants lifting their hands when they sing. It seems weird to first-time visitors and can feel uncomfortable. What are they doing and why?

Lifting our hands is an act of surrender of our will. God is holy and is the Supreme Authority. It's our way of telling God that we recognize who He is and that He can move in and take control of the issues we're praying for in our lives. Raising our hands is a physical act of praise and worship and of humbling ourselves before Him, as is bowing our heads or kneeling.

Some believers may even fall face down on the floor when they pray. They want God to see their complete submission. These prayer stances are not only done for Him but for us. They open our spirit up, allowing God's Spirit to enter into our lives to work in deeper dimensions.

■ ■ ■

How much have you surrendered to Him? Learn to take the stance of submission in His presence. Raise up your hands, bow, and kneel. He is holy and worthy to be praised.

Day 3

BE WARY OF PREDATORS

For they mouth empty, boastful words and, by appealing to
the lustful desires of the flesh, they entice people who
are just escaping from those who live in error.

2 PETER 2:18

*O*ver the years of living and working in Hollywood, I've
seen lots of desperate individuals who've given up everything to follow their dream of becoming a star. Many have
left families and successful careers, hoping to cash in on fame
and fortune.

Spiritual cults prey upon and entrap people desperate for
stardom. One in particular tells Hollywood dreamers they need
to improve their minds, claiming their scientific methods will
allow them to fulfill their dreams. The leaders of this global cult
use manipulation. They've even built a center to allure unsuspecting actors and those wanting to break into the industry by
offering free coaching and career advice.

Second Peter 2:19 says, "They promise them freedom, while
they themselves are slaves of depravity—for 'people are slaves
to whatever has mastered them.'" Our culture is full of places to
be deceived. Cults will continue to prey on our desires, leading
us into disastrous choices. God's Word is a "lamp unto our feet
and a light onto our paths." (Psalm 119:105). Stay in it and be
wary of predators.

■ ■ ■

*Have you let your selfish desires enticed you into a wrong kind of
lifestyle? How could you help others from falling into the deception?*

Day 4

PRESENCE

The LORD replied, "My Presence will go with you,
and I will give you rest."

EXODUS 33:14

*H*er eyes were as blue as the sky, and she had a presence that was penetrating. Our hearts met instantly. We were sisters of God. I was in Israel filming, and Sister Elizabeth was a sequestered nun, one of only a few who were allowed outside the walls at St. Mary of the Resurrection Abbey, located in the heavily populated Muslim community of Abu Ghosh.

St. Mary's is part of the Benedictine monastery located on top of Roman ruins. It is said to be the site of the city of Emmaus, where Jesus met two of his disciples after His resurrection. Archaeologists can trace human presence there for 6,000 years. The nuns (and monks) start their day at 3:00 a.m. with prayer and Bible reading, maintain the grounds, and do what they can to provide for their minimal needs. They have a keen awareness of God's presence in other people and it was evident in my conversation with Sister Elizabeth.

As I entered the small shop to purchase some of the art they create at St. Mary's, I was overwhelmed with the presence of God. As we shared, God's presence enveloped the sister and radiated out to me. Our spiritual souls locked with each other and there was an instant bond. When God fills our lives, it is felt mutually. There is a supernatural connection. I got a glimpse of heaven at that moment. We will know Him and know our brothers and sisters in God's kingdom.

■ ■ ■

How do those you meet on the roads of life sense God's presence when they meet you?

Journal

WEEK

Day 1

PRESSURIZED

I pray that out of his glorious riches he may strengthen
you with power through his Spirit in your inner being.

EPHESIANS 3:16

When scuba diving, my ears have to equalize with the water's pressure, so I descend very slowly. I hold my nose and blow out through my ears, breathing slow and steady as I keep my eyes open to the unknown watery environment I'm descending into.

Similarly, we need to pressurize ourselves in our daily lives. It's easy to feel panicky over the constant uncertainty of world events and life's pressures. Our soul needs to pressurize to God's world and slowly breathe in God's oxygen. He's our regulator—our air supply. As we descend into the depths of the unknown, our eyes should be open to what He wants to show us and where He wants to take us

I also strap on a buoyancy control device (BCD vest) and an air tank to keep me afloat and breathing underwater. In the same way, we need to strap on God's buoyancy vest of prayer and His oxygen tank of Scripture. They give us the ability and power to breathe in a world that's full of unknown obstacles. If you find yourself sinking into deep water, gear up, blow out the cares of this world, and breathe in God's oxygen. He's going to take you to find treasures unknown.

■ ■ ■

What pressures are surrounding you today? Breathe in God's life-giving oxygen as you sink into the depths of life's complicated and unknown world.

Day 2

PRIORITIES

"But seek first his kingdom and his righteousness,
and all these things will be given to you as well."

MATTHEW 6:33

"*I* have so much to do! I just need to do one more thing and then I can sit down and spend time today with you, Father." I was too busy and unable to slow down. I'm as guilty as anyone. It's my desire to prioritize my God time each day, so why don't I? Why do I let distractions get in the way? Is your "one more thing" keeping you from all the things you desire? How can we stop the noise of "need to do" for the peace of "must do"? God's told us if we want all that good stuff, we have to seek Him first.

Interestingly, on those days when I catch myself finding one more thing to do, my day is scattered and I don't get much done. But when I prioritize my time with Him, I'm focused and able to accomplish much more. It's a mystery how it works, but my time seems to expand. It really comes down to our will—our will to follow His priorities instead of ours

Christian music, podcasts on leadership, and YouTube talks won't take the place of being with the Source of all we want in life. If we can get this right, all the other priorities—the other issues—won't matter..

■ ■ ■

Have you written God time into your schedule? What's your "one more thing" that's keeping you from Him? Write down your excuses so you don't use them.

Day 3

HEAVENLY PROTECTION

"Because he loves me," says the LORD, "I will rescue him;
I will protect him, for he acknowledges my name."

PSALM 91:14

I was seven months pregnant when my husband fell out of a helicopter. He was filming in Kingston, Jamaica, and had rented a helicopter to get a crowd shot of the thousands of people who were coming to pack the stadium that night. The helicopter wasn't set up for filming, so they took the doors off and tied Phil in with a rope, which we later found out was too long.

As they lifted off, he was hanging off the side, with his feet on the landing skid as he held a camera (they were much larger and heavier in the '80s). That's when the pilot made a quick turn, and Phil, who wasn't holding on, fell forward and out the door. Fortunately, the pilot saw him and, thinking quickly, turned sharply in the opposite direction, throwing him back inside the helicopter. God had protected him.

We do some wild and crazy things in life, and I've wondered how often our heavenly Father sends His angels to sustain and protect us. When we get to heaven, I think we'll find out He sent lots of angels. In life we are never prepared for those moments that seem to have been well planned out and then turn tragic. But God has His eyes on us. Trust Him. He had Phil's back that night, and He has yours too.

■ ■ ■

What crazy situation has God saved you from? Read Psalm 91 and be encouraged that God is watching out for His children.

Day 4

PUSHING THE SEND KEY

> David also said to Solomon his son, "Be strong and
> courageous, and do the work. Do not be afraid or
> discouraged, for the LORD God, my God, is with you.
> He will not fail you or forsake you until all the work for
> the service of the temple of the LORD is finished."
>
> 1 CHRONICLES 28:20

cofounded a women's conference in Los Angeles called
ASCEND. God orchestrated the daunting task, and in ret-
rospect I marvel at how He provided and the lessons I learned.
Those leadership lessons are a foundation I continue to build on.
ASCEND launched me into new God-given tasks, but I had to
push the Send key and give God permission to use me and then
step aside eventually so God could send someone else.

David was launching Solomon to build God's temple. What
a daunting task Solomon had been assigned by God to do. It
was one that David had wanted for himself, but God had not
ordained it. David had to trust God and let God send Solomon.

Sometimes God will ask us to do things and we have to be
willing. Other times we have to send others. While the idea or
vision may be God given, we may not be the one God chooses to
complete it. What David didn't understand was that if it hadn't
been for his fatherly direction and encouragement in Solomon's
life, Solomon wouldn't have had the drive to complete God's
daunting task. He needed David to push the Send key.

■ ■ ■

*What task has God asked you to do, but you're hovering over the Send
key? Determine to hit the key today.*

Journal

WEEK

39

Day 1

POST GRACE

Therefore let us stop passing judgment on one another.
Instead, make up your mind not to put any stumbling block
or obstacle in the way of a brother or sister.

ROMANS 14:13

We're a culture of quick studies and decision-makers. People take mere seconds to decide if they want to listen to someone. As a media producer and consultant, I'm always educating clients on how to grab people's attention quickly, especially on social media platforms. Pictures and words matter. The downside is that we've become an overly critical and judgmental culture. And on social media, people get vicious, even those who call themselves Christians.

As believers in Christ, we need to be extra careful with our words. Humor and sarcasm can produce laughs, but can also backfire and build impenetrable spiritual walls. People form perceptions not only about you and other Christians but, most importantly, about God.

The word *Christian* means "little Christ." Are you being a "little Christ" when you send pictures and make comments? God's Word stands by itself. You don't need to defend it with angry comments. Images and words can be divisive tools of the enemy; don't let him win. Let's get the culture's attention by being Christians known on social media for reflecting God's grace and mercy.

■ ■ ■

When was the last time you regretted something you posted on social media? Always think before you hit that Post button and be sure you're sending grace.

Day 2

THREE REQUIREMENTS

He has shown you, O mortal, what is good. And what
does the LORD require of you? To act justly and
to love mercy and to walk humbly with your God.

MICAH 6:8

*W*atching over someone as they die and not being able
to help is so very difficult. Especially when that person is suffering. It truly is emotionally excruciating. Doctors,
nurses, and other hospice caregivers are earthly angels, as are
humanitarian aid workers, who must watch people, especially
children, die of starvation or infectious diseases.

What does God require of us? How can we function when
we see suffering people all around us? God asks us to do three
things, but they aren't achievable without Him. We have to act
justly, love mercy, and walk humbly with Him. Jesus was the
only man to walk the earth who succeeded in these three areas,
and it was because of the perfection of Jesus that God was able
to accept Him as a perfect sacrifice for our sin.

God can't take us out of the suffering, broken world we're
condemned to live our days in, but Jesus is the reason we never
have to suffer alone. In the midst of excruciating suffering, His
presence is with us, and we're able to endure.

■ ■ ■

*How can you act justly, love mercy, and walk humbly with God?
Make three columns and title them Justice, Mercy, and Humility.
Then list some practical ways you can follow these three instructions.*

Day 3

RESTORATION

"And I will bring my people Israel back from exile.
They will rebuild the ruined cities and live in them.
They will plant vineyards and drink their wine;
they will make gardens and eat their fruit."

AMOS 9:14

She came to Dubai as a model. She was also a believer in Jesus Christ, and she knew her true beauty and identity was in Him. Working in a predominately Muslim culture was challenging, but she respected it. Even so, her beauty kept putting her in high-profile places, often with wealthy men.

One admirer was completely mesmerized by her beauty and wanted to date her—even possess her. She was kind in her responses to his aggressive advances, but finally had to be firm in denying his demands. She confessed that she was a Christian and although she'd like to be friends, she couldn't enter a romantic relationship with a nonbeliever. The next day, as she was entering a building for a modeling job, he came out from a hiding place and threw acid on her face, destroying it and forever changing the course of her life.

Miles from the support of family and with no one to help her, she prayed. Amazingly God sent a wealthy Muslim family who'd heard of the horrific incident. They were Good Samaritans, paying for her multiple surgeries and taking care of her as she healed. In the process, they witnessed her complete forgiveness of her assailant and came to know her Jesus, the Redeemer of our lives. What was done as evil, God turned to good.

■ ■ ■

How has God brought restoration in your life? Trust Him, and go bring hope to someone today.

Day 4

RESTORING TRUST

> Who may ascend into the hill of the LORD?
> And who may stand in His holy place? He who has
> clean hands and a pure heart, who has not lifted up
> his soul to falsehood and has not sworn deceitfully.
>
> PSALM 24:3–4 NASB

She'd hurt me yet again. I had trusted her to do the right thing, and I got burned. This time it had left a scar not just on me but also on my child. I'd forgive her, but I couldn't trust her again. But God was asking me to. *What? Really, Lord?* I heard His small voice say, "You've hurt and left scars on others. Look at my feet and hands."

God's grace and mercy is incomprehensible. He made us in His image, and our heart's desire is to mirror His, but with some people it seems impossible. How can we restore trust and erase the scars?

We can't. Jesus still had scars on His hands and feet when He rose from the dead. But they weren't painful anymore; His pain and suffering had been worth the redemption and restoration of His most precious possession—us. When we forgive but don't allow the rebuilding process of trust, wholehearted healing can't be completed. It's our trust that helps people trust in themselves again. How many times do we have to forgive? Jesus tells us in Matthew 18:22, "Seventy-seven times."

∎ ∎ ∎

Who's hurt you that you've forgiven but failed to allow trust to be restored? Ask God to build your trust back. Is it scary? You bet, but their full recovery and yours may depend on it.

Journal

WEEK

40

Day 1

RESTRAINED FREEDOM

Let us also lay aside every weight,
and the sin which clings so closely, and let us run
with endurance the race that is set before us.

HEBREWS 12:1 ESV

*S*ome of the freest people I've ever met have endured life circumstances where they've been restrained in some way. Temple Grandin is an autistic savant and the subject of a wonderful film by the same name produced in 2010. She has a keen ability to see things and calculate them, but she's also restricted by her autism. She's thrown into uncontrollable convulsions, which limits her ability to function.

As a child, she spent summers working on her family's cattle ranch and would help brand cattle by corralling them into a restraint system. She noticed that the cattle would go into a complete frenzy while waiting, but as soon as they entered the restraint box, they calmed. Knowing how her body uncontrollably shook because of her autism, she put herself into the cattle's restraint box one day. The restraint brought immediate peace and calmness, and she could gain control over her body by sitting in the box for long periods of time. Now, the "squeeze machine" or "hug box" is used in many autism care facilities around the world.

Obedience (often viewed as restraint) brings freedom if we're willing. When you're suffering—not getting your way or getting your prayers answered—count it as joy and be at peace. God uses our quieted spirit to teach profound truths. He's grooming and branding you as His own.

■ ■ ■

What do you want from God? Count three ways you can restrain yourself and be obedient. Then see how it frees you.

NOISY MINDS

Therefore, with minds that are alert and fully sober,
set your hope on the grace to be brought to you
when Jesus Christ is revealed at his coming.

1 PETER 1:13

The world is a noisy place. I've read that restaurants purposefully want their establishments to be loud because patrons feel that noisy restaurants are successful—hip and cool. Noisy restaurants also cause us to eat and drink more and to "party on."

Headphone or earbud wires decorate people like a new kind of jewelry today. The top Christmas request by adults in 2016 was wireless headphones. We use our mobile devices to pump music or other content into our ears to escape boredom and fill the time. Headphones block out those around us so we don't have to confront them, and allow us to zone out in subways, airplanes, gyms, and any place we go.

Oftentimes, we use the outside noise of our devices to drown the inside noise of our souls. We're afraid of hearing our thoughts. Thoughts that might make us feel guilty or ashamed. Thoughts of why we're on this planet and what will happen when we die. And we're drowning out God's ability to answer those questions. Constant noise in our ears keeps us from confronting God, who wants to deal with our issues so He can bring peace to our restless souls. Before God can bring you hope, though, you must be able to hear Him.

■ ■ ■

Take out your earphones and go for a walk, ride your bike, or lay down on the grass outside and look up. God's ready to talk are you? Are you listening?

Day 3

GRADUATING TO KNOWLEDGE

My people are destroyed from lack of knowledge.
"Because you have rejected knowledge, I also reject you
as my priests; because you have ignored the law
of your God, I also will ignore your children."

HOSEA 4:6

My daughter's high school principal told me she was bored with her classmates' level of thinking. He was worried she'd lose direction and make some poor choices, so he suggested that my husband and I allow her to graduate early, at sixteen years of age. To cover the required courses, she enrolled in a local community college, or, as she put it, "high school with ashtrays."

We're overwhelmed with information today and it's making us thoughtless, and causing intelligent people to make bad choices. Lack of time keeps us from turning information into wisdom.

God's punishment for the children of Israel, who allowed their thoughts to be diverted, was harsh and their children followed their choices and habits. God disciplined them but even more devastating, God disciplined their children. We're to be cautious of the content we're choosing and how much time we spend on needless information and entertainment or we will only be going from high school to high school with ashtrays—adults whose thinking never develops. Kingdom-minded thought leaders are needed in a culture that hungers for direction. Scripture tells us we're to avoid "godless chatter" (2 Timothy 2:16).

■ ■ ■

How might you change the media content you're consuming and adjust how much time you're spending on it? God gave us His book—the Word—to study, but it's up to us to change our school of thinking.

KNOWN

For the earth will be filled with the knowledge
of the glory of the LORD as the waters cover the sea.

HABAKKUK 2:14

We're living in the information age, with an avalanche of content and data delivered to us via satellites and the Internet as never before in history. What was once an impossibility—to reach *every* person on earth at one time with information and knowledge—has now virtually been achieved.

God reveals Himself to us in word (the Bible) and in sight (through nature). His creation speaks to our souls even if we ignore His written Word. Even creation recognizes God. When Jesus had his triumphal entry into Jerusalem, he said if the people were silent, "the stones along the road would burst into cheers" (Luke 19:40 NLT). Satan's ultimate goal is to mislead souls for eternity.

God said His earth has been filled with His knowledge as deep as the sea, and He promises that one day "every knee will bow before me; every tongue will acknowledge God" (Romans 14:11). Technology has made it possible, so we have no excuse not to know Him. His knowledge has been made known and clear, if we're willing to seek Him honestly.

■ ■ ■

How are you helping to further the knowledge of God? Create an intriguing question that you could ask someone to make them search for true knowledge. That's what Jesus did.

Journal

WEEK

41

Day 1

PRAYER SUPPORTS

Calling the Twelve to him, he began to send them out
two by two and gave them authority over impure spirits.

MARK 6:7

*I*s God calling you on a special journey or mission? Don't go alone. God has promised that He goes before us if we walk in His will (Deuteronomy 31:6), but He also wants us to take a support person. In fact, He empowers us when we bring company, giving us authority (Matthew 18:20).

I consider Hollywood my mission field. I've seen many Christians come to the city of their dreams only to lose their footing in Christ because they tried to do it with no support. The Hollywood Prayer Network, whose board I serve on, has a mission to pray for and support Christian media and entertainment professionals in Hollywood. We recognize the importance of a support system, especially in one of the most influential industries in the world. Too often, Christians have criticized Hollywood rather than choosing to pray for those who work on the inside. But we've seen lives preserved and changed, and God's army of believers is growing in Hollywood. But we still need more prayer and support.

When God plants on your heart a calling and mission, trust Him to prepare the hearts and lives of those around you to walk the road with you. God doesn't want you going it alone.

■ ■ ■

Have you ever prayed for the Christian professionals in Hollywood? Do it today and then as God calls you to your mission, ask Him to provide prayer supporters for you.

Day 2

FEAR HORNS

The LORD is my light and my salvation—whom shall I fear?
The LORD is the stronghold of my life—
of whom shall I be afraid?

PSALM 27:1

When I traveled to India for the first time, I was told that "India is an assault on your senses." I knew I would see and smell unusual things, but I wasn't prepared for the constant sound of honking cars, buses, trucks, and motorcycles. There aren't traffic lanes in India, just suggestions. Bicycles, motorcycles, and tut-tuts squeeze into any available space between the vehicles, so drivers must constantly warn other vehicles around them of their presence by honking. The fear of being hit takes control of their honking trigger finger and they honk even when there is no reason to. The noisy streets throughout India become deafening and numbing to the soul over time. You long for quiet when you leave the country.

Fear can become a habit. We get so used to living with it that we no longer recognize its deafening noise—its grip in our lives. But Jesus came that we might have peace. He conquered the greatest of all fears—death. Trust Him for whatever it is that you fear.

Jesus is in the midst of your jammed pathways, so there's no need to honk. He sees where you are. Fear not.

■ ■ ■

What fear has you honking? Let God's stronghold of peace take control.

SIMPLE PLEASURES

The righteous has enough to satisfy his appetite,
but the stomach of the wicked is in need.

PROVERBS 13:25 NASB

*T*he ice cream dripped down the cone onto her little fingers as she blissfully licked her first ice cream cone, pronouncing that it was "so … good!" And the oldies radio station played a tune about sitting on the dock of the bay wasting time while we giggled the afternoon away. These are cherished memory moments with great laughter.

Have we lost moments of profound simplicity, wonder, and joy? In our hamster-wheel lives, have we forgotten how to be content with an appetite that truly has enough? Our plates are filled with must-dos because we "can do" so much more. We can't stop devouring the dots like an endless Pac-Man game. How do we hold onto a contented simple life in a world of moving targets and an endless marathon race for bigger and better? What's the cure, and how do we jump off the spinning wheel and end the game?

We look up. We refuse what the world promises as a blue-plate special of happiness and instead choose God's plate of lasting joy that satisfies the longings of our hearts. We determine to stop taking more and instead start giving more, and then sit in His presence for a bit. It's "so … good."

■ ■ ■

Find three ways today to simplify your life. Then think of three people who could use encouragement. Handwrite three notes of thanks to them for just being themselves. Send simple love.

Day 4

CLEAR VISION

For all that is in the world, the lust of the flesh
and the lust of the eyes and the boastful pride of life,
is not from the Father, but is from the world.

1 JOHN 2:16 NASB

*A*s I have aged, I have become visually challenged. So I navigate life in monovision. I wear a contact lens in my left eye to see things up close, and I use my right eye (without a lens) to view things off in the distance. Each eye works separately, and my brain seamlessly tells my eyes which one to use according to what I'm looking at. But, if I don't have my left contact lens in, I'm visually impaired and I miss small details.

God is my contact lens in life. If He's in my sight, I know He'll keep me going in the right direction. He stops me from running into walls, like deceptions, and keeps my sight clear and focused on His purposes. When I don't insert Him into my vision, then I see only those distant things with my lens-free eye. My sinful nature searches outwardly for worldly desires and I end up wandering without clear vision.

God wants us to see His clear and perfect vision for our lives. But we have to insert His lens into our eye daily and trust Him.

■ ■ ■

Has God brought a new focus in your life? If so, what is it? Insert God's high-powered lens and see even more of what He wants to show you.

Journal

SMALL BITES

I gave you milk, not solid food, for you were not yet
ready for it. Indeed, you are still not ready.

1 CORINTHIANS 3:2

*W*hile in Spain, I enjoyed tapas—small plates of food.
These gourmet dishes are trendy today. In fact, the
snack industry exploded several years ago when it started pack-
aging cookies and crackers into bite-sized pieces. Manufacturers
discovered we actually consume more that way, and their profits
skyrocketed.

I believe if we're going to expose people to the gospel today,
we have to offer it in small bites. Otherwise, they have a hard
time digesting God's rich truths and the grace of His redemptive message in one gulp. Nonbelievers have been exposed to
an overabundance of false information and deceptive lies, so
spiritual thought needs to be introduced to them like intriguing
appetizers. They have had a steady diet of rhetoric and don't
want to risk possible heartburn. They have observed and some
have tasted false doctrines, cults, and religious schemes, keeping them wary of God's banquet table.

So how can we offer the life-saving Bread of Life—Jesus—
to them? How can we inject the sweetness of God into starving
lives? By creating small bites—little things we do and say that
create small introductions to God's love, grace, and mercy. We
bring little loving samples that garnish their lives with a taste of
Jesus. Start with a plate of Word tapas from Proverbs.

■ ■ ■

*Prepare three tasty small bites—simple acts of love. Make them in-
triguing and offer them to someone today. Ask thoughtful questions
and share a morsel of your personal story.*

SOMEWHERE IT'S SNOWING

Blessed is the one whose transgressions are forgiven,
whose sins are covered.

PSALM 32:1

*S*now is a beautiful creation of God. It covers the drab, dirty environment with a clean white covering of freshness. It brings silence as it muffles sound, and despite its inconvenience and sometimes overabundance, it can bring pure joy.

I had the privilege to attend college with David Stearman, writer of the song "Somewhere It's Snowing."[33] From the first time I heard the words he had written, they brought me a renewed understanding of God's grace—that forgiveness, like snow, covers us.

David compared snow to the way God covers our sin with His grace. Grace that covers our multitude of sins and brings peace. It cleans up our messes and freshens and renews our hope. It quiets our fears and turns tears to joy. It allows us to approach God with confidence and not shame—shame that sometimes keeps us forever from God. Hebrews 4:16 says, "Let us then approach God's throne of grace with confidence, so that we may receive mercy and find grace to help us in our time of need."

You are forgiven. God did it on the cross. Somewhere it's snowing, so let God's grace and mercy bring a fresh covering into your life today.

■ ■ ■

Who in your life needs some "snow"—God's grace? Take the good news of God's forgiveness to them today.

Day 3

SHEPHERDS NEEDED

"Return, faithless people," declares the LORD, "… I will give
you shepherds after my own heart, who will lead you
with knowledge and understanding."

JEREMIAH 3:14 –15

We've seen reports of the thousands of refugees flooding out of cities in the Middle East over recent years. In many cases, they've been forced to leave the homes they have occupied with their families for generations. Many countries have taken them in, but local people who fear the refugees have put political pressure on their government leaders in these sanctuary cities. Worried about how the large numbers of people are going to change their cultures, they're pushing for the refugees to be sent back.

But God is doing something interesting. As the refugees come in, so are their broken hearts and spiritual lives. They're hungry for spiritual truth, and thousands have begun to follow Jesus. Many who've been working with the refugees are scrambling to find spiritual shepherds—Bible teachers for the thousands of new believers. The refugees aren't just asking for physical food and clothing, but for biblical instruction. They're desperate to grow in their new faith.

With the ongoing fear, the refugees may soon be forced to return to their bombed-out cities. As new believers, they want to be prepared for what may come: more persecution and perhaps even death. So more than physical provisions, they're desperate for spiritual provision.

■ ■ ■

Pray about the refugee crisis in our world today. How might you be able to show God's love and shepherd those who are desperate for God?

DEMONIC SPIRITS

Submit yourselves, then, to God. Resist the devil,
and he will flee from you.

JAMES 4:7

*O*ne of William Shakespeare's most famous plays is *The
Tragedy of Macbeth*, which depicts the physical and psy-
chological effects of ambition and the desire for power. Lady
Macbeth talks her husband into killing the king of Scotland so
he will gain the throne.

One of the most well-known lines comes while Lady
Macbeth is being observed by the doctor and gentlewoman,
who are worried she'll commit suicide (which she eventually
does), as she's being haunted by guilt. They watch her as she
rubs her hands as if washing them, saying, "Out, damned spot!
Out, I say! ... Hell is murky." Interestingly, the doctor says she
needs more of "the divine than the physician."[34] In other words,
she needs the power of God to rid her of her demons.

The devil and his demons can and do haunt us. If we believe the Bible, we have to believe in the reality of satan. Do
you know how to resist them? God tells us to submit ourselves
to God and call on the name of Jesus. God has authority over
heaven and hell. Trying to ignore demons or telling them to go
away without the name of Jesus does nothing. You need "the divine"—the Great Physician.

■ ■ ■

*When was a time that you felt the oppression of demonic spirits? The
next time it happens, use the name of Jesus.*

Journal

WEEK

43

Day 1

SPRINGS WITHOUT WATER

These are springs without water and mists driven by a storm,
for whom the black darkness has been reserved.

2 PETER 2:17 NASB

*L*as Vegas means "the meadows" because in the middle of the dry, desolate desert, beneath the hard ground, lie underground water sources. For years, Las Vegas, Nevada, was only a watering stop for Native Americans, pioneers, stagecoaches, and eventually trains. No one wanted to settle in what seemed like God-forsaken land. The fertile lands of California lay ahead, and few were crazy enough to stay in Las Vegas until the first casino was built in 1931.

Growing up in Las Vegas, I became well acquainted with the results of springs of dry water. It's called liquor, and it promises a diversion from life's misery. However, this momentary panacea only made people thirst for more damaging and devastating substances.

Jesus said, "Let anyone who is thirsty come to me to drink" (John 7:37). Excessive liquor or other addictive substances used by satan, the deceiver, will never solve our suffering. They will only lead to disastrous darkness, as they numb our ability to make life-giving choices.

Each of us have challenges and vices, whether they be alcohol, drugs, tobacco, money, fame, or (for me) sugar. We all must choose how to resist the "springs without water" that are placed before us daily. We must drink Jesus' living water. He's the one and only source for satisfaction.

■ ■ ■

What are some of your vices? Have a drink of Jesus, and allow Him to bring life in the barren and forsaken places within you.

Day 2

STOP BEATING YOURSELF UP

> You will keep in perfect peace those whose
> minds are steadfast, because they trust in you.
>
> ISAIAH 26:3

*A*lexander Pope, an English poet and the translator of Homer, once said, "To err is human."[35] In today's culture, failure doesn't seem to be an option; it's certainly not what we want to post on our social media pages. Our culture pushes us to be superhuman.

In multiple stories in the Bible, God taught leaders that failure can be fixable—if we're willing to learn from our failings and move on. He gives second chances. He teaches us to trust Him and not forget that a strong *listening* relationship to God keeps our feet on a secure and steady path. Peace and success prevails when our minds are focused on His goals, not ours.

Do you need to recover from failure and change directions? Stop beating yourself up, dust yourself off, and regroup. Stop talking negatively to yourself. God's living *with* you if you allow Him to take control of your life. Don't say, "I'm so stupid," or "I'm an idiot!" Change those to, "Okay, I had a bit of a stumble. What did I miss, God? Forgive me and show me how to move through it with *your* guidance and not my will."

"To err *is* human," but God brings redemption and a way back. Put your trust in Him.

■ ■ ■

How do you criticize yourself? Stop and rethink it. Memorize the verse above. It's a promise of peace and of a clear and strong mind— His mind.

Day 3

VIRTUAL REALITY OR HISTORICAL BIBLICAL STORIES?

Jesus answered: "Watch out that no one deceives you."

MATTHEW 24:4

Hollywood storytellers are keen to use the latest technology (like virtual reality) to make their stories even more real for their audiences. They love great stories and they're passionate about making them come alive. Over the years, many nonbelieving filmmakers, looking to make a buck, have taken Bible stories and interpreted them on the big screen, knowing they have great plots and can make interesting films. The results have sometimes been good and sometimes not so good.

Most movies made by Hollywood aren't true, but Bible stories are. The flood, the parting of the Red Sea, David killing Goliath, and Jesus' miracles, like changing water into wine and healing the sick, aren't Hollywood magic or special effects. They actually happened. So how can we educate our children to know the difference between fictional stories (like *Harry Potter*, *Star Wars*, and *Hunger Games*) and biblical accounts? We have to read and know the Bible for ourselves.

"Watch out." That is the instruction that Jesus gave us because it's easy to be deceived especially with the technological magic we have available to us today. Take the time to learn and teach your children by making sure they know the real stories of the Bible and call them that—not just a stories. They're Bible stories based on actual *historical* events. Don't be deceived.

■ ■ ■

What is your favorite story in the Bible, and why? Share it with someone today.

Day 4

HUMBLY STRIP DOWN

"If anyone wants to sue you and take your shirt,
hand over your coat as well. If anyone forces you to go a mile,
go with them two miles."

MATTHEW 5:40–41

*I*nvisible. That's how they felt. The Roman government had taxed the Jews so severely that everything but the shirts on their backs had been taken. To maintain their decadent lifestyles, Roman government land owners took their entire possessions mercilessly. The cost of living along with high taxes was so exorbitant that the everyday person couldn't escape poverty. Sound familiar?

Jesus was raised in poverty—an economic and political stranglehold. The Jews either cowered and gave up trying, or they fought back—usually destructively. They felt stuck. Jesus taught us to take a stand in a godly way—to strip down. When evil creditors come knocking, go to a public place (social media) and humbly give them everything. Expose them to your nothingness. Even more so, go above and beyond to assist the evildoer. Does is sound absurd? Why would Jesus tell us to do that? Humiliation.

In today's culture of social media, humiliation is frequent. It is often the weapon of choice. But Jesus also warns that using humiliation for revenge is equally wrong. Jesus said to "love your enemies and pray for those who persecute you, that you may be children of your Father in heaven" (Matthew 40:44–45). When we're up against difficult situations, we must choose the right spirit, approaching others humbly but wisely.

■ ■ ■

Next time you want to fight back or cower away, stand up God's way. He will bless you for your obedience.

Journal

WEEK

Day 1

THINKING TRAPS

The fear of the LORD is the beginning of knowledge,
but fools despise wisdom and instruction.

PROVERBS 1:7

*M*any times, the viewpoints presented by journalists, celebrities, and other media sources sound logical. But we're so gullible that we fall into thinking traps and don't even know it. What's tragic is that we can become blind fools and end up defending false wisdom as truth.

Anther trap of our rapid-fire media industry today is its ability to take an individual partial statement or opinion and manipulate it to have a completely different meaning. Consequently, Christian leaders have been made to look like fools. Before opening their mouth, they didn't investigate thoroughly or think about how the public might interpret their statements and opinions. The public gets the impression that all Christians think the same way, resulting in a huge negative PR problem in the United States.

Both examples come from a lack of learning to think. What's sad is that many times individuals know it's wrong but still do it. The reasons are many, but next time you're ready to give an opinion in public, ask yourself, if God were standing right next to you, would He agree with you or slap you down? And don't forget to also check your arrogance at the door. Wise up and fear God.

■ ■ ■

Stop and think the next time something controversial comes your way. Write down three ways you can check your facts.

Day 2

SUBSTANCE ABUSE

They exchanged the truth about God for a lie,
and worshiped and served created things rather than
the Creator—who is forever praised.

ROMANS 1:25

*W*e consume lots of junk food in America, and I'm just as guilty as anyone. We also consume another kind of junk—junk media and entertainment. In 2016, Neilson reported in the *New York Times* that on average, people consume ten hours and thirty-nine minutes of media content daily on their combined devices.[36] Most of us sleep far less than that. Our appetite for media is affecting our lives. Are you watching anything worthwhile or of real substance? Or are you just allowing junk media and entertainment to take over your mind and put you in a media coma?

Our souls need God and His nourishment just as our bodies need healthy food. In our culture today, we've become addicted to noise and media diversions. If we keep something playing in our ears all the time, we can continue to ignore God's direction. So our media cravings control us while God's voice and truths get muted. Maybe it's time to shut down some channels and listen to Jesus instead.

■ ■ ■

Calculate the amount of time you spend on junk media and entertainment. How do you think it's affecting your relationship with God?

Day 3

SWEET AROMA

For we are to God the pleasing aroma of Christ among those
who are being saved and those who are perishing.

2 CORINTHIANS 2:15

When I slept at my grandmother Mimi's house, the smell of her French crepes always woke me in the morning. I knew she'd been up since dawn making my favorite treat on earth. In my mind, I can still smell their sweet aroma today.

I was fortunate to grow up in a safe and secure environment in the United States. My childhood years were much different from Mimi's. She had immigrated to America as a teenager in the early 1900s, having lived in poverty for much of her life. For this reason, she taught me to prepare for the unpredictable and that the only lasting security in life is to be anchored in Jesus Christ. His love and security were her key ingredients for living a contented life.

Mimi taught me that a contented life could be built by taking each turn of events—those unpredictable occurrences—and finding God's joy in the simplicity of basic things. He blesses us each day with His delicious treats and wants us to share His love and hope with the busy and uncertain world we live in.

People are perishing around the globe as they flee dangerous situations, but in the midst of that hopelessness we can be a sweet aroma of Christ. The world needs the love of Jesus. In the rush of your day, don't miss those moments when you can tell someone of His saving grace.

■ ■ ■

How have you passed on your personal recipe for living courageously?
Be a memorable sweet aroma of Jesus today.

SWIMMING WITH DAD

When you pass through the waters,
I will be with you; and when you pass through the rivers,
they will not sweep over you.

ISAIAH 43:2

*F*or many summers my dad was a lifeguard for a private beach at Donner Lake, California. Donner, my favorite place on earth, is in the beautiful Sierra Nevada Mountains, and it is known for its crystal-clear lake and breathtaking scenery. I was a fearless toddler, so my mom had to keep a keen eye on me as I would head straight for the deep water where my dad was swimming. I wanted to be out there with him.

In my personal spiritual life, I always want to be swimming with my heavenly Father, but there have been times I've felt as if I couldn't get to Him. He was in the deep water, and I was stuck on the shore. Have you ever felt that way? Weighed down with life's challenges, it can feel as if something's always holding us back. But if we start to sink, Jesus throws us a life preserver. He's there with outstretched arms, ready to lift us up and put us back onto dry land.

Jesus swam with the suffering and the broken, and never turned away from the needy; He swam out into their deep waters. If we want to reach Jesus, we had better be good swimmers and be comfortable with big waves, which means knowing how to reach out to those who are drowning. We need to be immersed in His Word so we can encourage others with His hope.

■ ■ ■

Memorize a new life-preserving Scripture today. Then share it with someone who is suffering.

Journal

WEEK

45

■ ■

Day 1

FEED THE SHEEP

Again Jesus said, "Simon son of John, do you love me?"
He answered, "Yes, Lord, you know that I love you."
Jesus said, "Take care of my sheep."

JOHN 21:16

Isabella Lilias Trotter (1853–1928) was a brilliant artist. *Many Beautiful Things* is a touching documentary that
chronicles Lilias's life and work as both an artist and missionary
in Algiers, Algeria, in Northern Africa. She was mentored by
one of the greatest artists of her time, John Ruskin, who promised her that if she would devote her life to art, she'd be a great
living artist and do immortal things. Most people would never
turn that opportunity down, but she did.

Why? She felt her art came easy to her, and God calls us
to go where it's difficult. She began to work in the ghettos of
London and discovered that her true purpose could be attained
only by giving sacrificially to others and helping them see they
were God's created beauty.

Lilias believed that choosing to follow an artistic career
would fulfill only half of what God wanted for her life. One of
the most beautiful aspects of her story is how her artistic work
flourished in North Africa in one of the most difficult places on
the planet. Her life paints a beautiful canvas for us today of faith
and surrender. To fully embrace all that God wants for us, we
have to care for His "sheep."

■ ■ ■

*What talents are you holding back that you need to surrender to
God? Think of three ways you can feed His sheep.*

TELL YOUR STORY

> With many similar parables Jesus spoke the word to them,
> as much as they could understand. He did not say anything
> to them without using a parable. But when he was alone
> with his disciples, he explained everything.
>
> MARK 4:33–34

*J*esus told stories and asked questions. So why aren't we doing the same? Stories ask us to believe. Jesus wants us to believe first with our hearts and then accept His teaching with our minds. His stories lead to thought-provoking questions. When someone asked Jesus a question, He almost always told a story or asked another question, offering explanations only to His disciples, not to the crowds that followed Him.

Our culture bombards us with thousands of media messages each day. We don't want anyone telling us what to think. We want to take in the information and decide for ourselves if it's truth or not. Information can always be argued and debated, but our personal journey—our stories—can't be. It's why your faith story with God is so important and should be told and written down for future generations.

The stories of Moses, Abraham, Esther, Ruth, David, and Jesus were first told and then written down. They will teach and enrich our lives until Jesus returns. Your personal story is valuable too. Hollywood has made billions of dollars on storytelling because stories reach our heart and are powerful influencers. Be bold and go tell stories.

■ ■ ■

What's your story? Write it down so you'll be prepared when a time comes to share it effectively.

Day 3

PREPARING FOR BATTLE

You will hear of wars and rumors of wars,
but see to it that you are not alarmed. Such things
must happen, but the end is still to come.

MATTHEW 24:6

*B*attles are raging in every area of our lives today. Wars are being waged physically, personally, politically, and ultimately spiritually. Jesus told us that He would one day return to earth and finish the final battle. We're to look for signs of His return, and one of them will be increasing battles. God doesn't want His children lost. But satan wants as many victims as he can deceive. So what are we to do while we wait?

Panic isn't an option. We're to prepare for the day when we may not have a physical Bible. Have you memorized Scripture? We're to prepare by uniting as a community of believers to support each other. Are you connected with a church or small group? We're to prepare our families. Are you teaching your children and grandchildren God's truths and promises? We're to prepare financially. Are you using your money wisely? We're also to prepare physically. Are you taking care of the body God has blessed you with and emotionally building muscle by finding assurance in your prayer time?

No one knows the hour or the day of Jesus' return, but preparation is half the battle.

■ ■ ■

What are you doing today to get prepared for Jesus' second coming?
Do what you need to, then help others prepare.

Day 4

THE CAREGIVER

These have come so that the proven genuineness of
your faith—of greater worth than gold, which perishes
even though refined by fire—may result in praise,
glory and honor when Jesus Christ is revealed.

1 PETER 1:7

On a hot Los Angeles day, I arrived early for a meeting. I needed time to pray and gather courage, as I'd been jarred by a door slamming on a project I'd spent months on. It felt as if I was standing with my face planted into a cement wall, but if I took one step back, I'd fall into an endless pit.

Across the parking lot, a caregiver from the assisted living facility pushed a frail woman in a wheelchair. Once the woman was positioned in a safe, sunny spot, the caregiver wrapped her in a blanket so she would feel comforted. I sat transfixed when God whispered into my heart, "That's me wrapping you up. You think you're almost dead, but I'm here with you in the heat of it all. I've made a way for you. I'm your Caregiver."

I entered my meeting a few minutes later, knowing the battle was already won. Miraculously, He made the cement wall fall just like the wall of Jericho. I'm still stunned by what happened—how He brought life to what I thought had died.

■ ■ ■

*What situation has you feeling as if you're going to fall into a pit?
Give it to the Caregiver and feel His presence.*

Journal

WEEK

ORDAINED DAYS

Your eyes saw my unformed body;
all the days ordained for me were written in your
book before one of them came to be.

PSALM 139:16

She should have died, but God's grace and a botched abortion saved her life. I sat at the luncheon, unable to stop the tears from flowing down my face. I've heard these stories for many years, but they move me every time. Mothers and children who have survived abortions. The joy of both is always overwhelmingly inspiring.

I'm a pro-lifer. I won't deny it. I believe all life is sacred, from conception till God's perfect timing for death. God's perfect plan for us was set into being before any of us were born. He has numbered our days, and the taking of life before His chosen time grieves His heart. Even so, His forgiveness is eternal.

We live in an inescapable fallen world—but it's also been redeemed by the blood of Jesus. What man intends for evil and destruction, God intends for good, bringing beauty from ashes. Each of us must choose how we want to control our lives. We all must choose how we will care for our bodies, minds, and hearts, and there are many ways to abuse them. Never forget that life is precious and valuable to God.

■ ■ ■

You are valuable. God knew you when you were still unformed, and He knows you now. What will you do with the life God's given you?

Day 2

BANISHING HOPELESSNESS

"Blessed are the poor in spirit,
for theirs is the kingdom of heaven."

MATTHEW 5:3

*Y*early, depression affects an estimated 350,000 people globally, and women are 70 percent more likely to experience depression than men.[37] Years ago I found myself in that dreaded gray fog. It was perplexing. I didn't have a perfect life, but God had blessed me and I had no obvious reasons to feel depressed. Thankfully, my doctor was able to quickly diagnose its root cause to a physical problem. But I'm now dependent on a daily thyroid pill.

When temporary blues creep in, it's important to find out if there is a medical reason, but it may mean we haven't spent enough time with our joy maker—God. When we focus on ourselves, what we *have* to do, places we *have* to go, and people we *have* to meet, our selfish desires rule our life. We're ungrateful for what God has done and the many ways He's enriched our lives.

Life is hard, but we can banish dreary days when we know how to fight them. If you're ever plagued with depression or self-doubt, remember how God has blessed you, which brings perspective. Then turn up the praise music. Physically singing praises to God releases our inner spirit to focus on Him. "God is our refuge and strength, an ever-present help in trouble" (Psalm 46:1). So don't lose hope.

■ ■ ■

What are the things you're truly thankful for in your life? Start a gratitude list, review it, and add to it often.

Day 3

A HANKERING

My soul is consumed with longing
for your laws at all times.

PSALM 119:20

*E*ver get a "hankering"—a craving that just pops into your head—for a chocolate chip cookie, a BBQ sandwich, or maybe a spa day? Our souls get hankerings too; they're cravings for God's order and peace. Those hankerings, or yearnings, come to us out of our innermost spiritual need for God. They're God's urgings, calling for us to connect with Him. Sometimes they pop into our heads because we yearn for discipline—to make better choices while satan tries to convince us otherwise.

Each year men and women sign up for military service because they've had a chaotic life with few rules. They long for consistency and order, and seek a military career to provide that. I've been told that once they leave the military and return to civilian life and a culture where rules matter less, they often return to a life of wandering. Many end up in prison where they're forced back into a culture of rules once again.

God has given us His truths of how to function in this world found in the Bible. Nature even teaches us a thing or two. The question is, are we listening to the yearnings—hankerings—of our soul for His truth and discipline? Or will we stay in denial, choosing to solve them with satan's deceptive answers? You choose.

■ ■ ■

What is your soul hankering for right now? Remember that God's truths keep us safe and flourishing in a world that struggles to find alternatives.

THE HEART KNOWS

His talk is smooth as butter, yet war is in his heart;
his words are more smoothing than oil,
yet they are drawn swords.

PSALM 55:21

*T*he director of our film leaned over to me as we were wrapping and said, "I've never had such a successful woman fix my coffee for me before." Jackie Green, the wife of Steve Green, president of Hobby Lobby, was making his coffee.

I'm always inspired by humble women who never call attention to themselves. When they see a need, they just get on with it. They're servants doing the will of their Father, and Jackie Green is one of them. She'll tell you that she's a dedicated wife and mother, but in reality she's so much more. Nothing is beneath her if God asks her to tackle it. She's been beside her husband, family, and company, inspiring them through monumental legal battles that have taken them to the United States Supreme Court.

If anyone's been around "smooth talkers" and "drawn swords," it's Jackie, but she battles with prayer, and the sword she swings in defense is the Bible. This is why she wants other people to know about its history, influence, and impact on the world. As a result, she and her husband have been the driving forces behind the Museum of the Bible in Washington, DC. This quiet, unassuming woman of God just does what God puts into her hands—and it all started with a Bible.

■ ■ ■

What humble thing has God called you to do? Are you doing it, or are you letting someone else step up and fix the coffee?

Journal

Day 1

THE INVITATION

"For many are invited, but few are chosen."
MATTHEW 22:14

*A*mid today's overbooked schedules, an invitation can be unwelcome. It may mean an infringement on time and finances (as with fundraising events, weddings, and birthdays) or an uncomfortable situation. Likewise, in our culture today, an invitation to become a member of God's kingdom might be looked at as an obligation rather than a liberation.

Read Matthew 22:1–14, the story surrounding the verse above, where a king tells his servants—a couple of times—to go "invite" people to a wedding. The invitees refuse, even killing the king's servants. The king retaliates, but unrelenting, he again sends out his servants to invite more people. When the king enters the event and sees an undressed guest, though, he throws him out. Sound puzzling?

God sends us invitations to come to Him, usually many times. Sometimes the messengers are destroyed—martyred. But God is relentless. He keeps sending out servants to invite ordinary people, outsiders, and the homeless. However, once they accept Him, He expects them to clean up their act—change their clothes, so to speak. God invites you to know Him, but He can't physically change you. You have to do that. You have to make the decision in your life to change your choices, attitudes, and habits. Hypocrites will be tossed out.

■ ■ ■

How do you view God's invitations? He's invited you in. What do you need to do to change your clothes?

THE KINGDOM CROWN TROPHY

Everyone who competes in the games goes into
strict training. They do it to get a crown that will not last,
but we do it to get a crown that will last forever.

1 CORINTHIANS 9:25

My dad spent hours teaching me the rules of all different sports games, but as an adult, football became
my favorite (thanks to my husband). Each year I look forward to
the college bowl games and especially the Super Bowl. However,
because we're in the media and commercial business, the Super
Bowl (the most watched TV program in the US) has taken on an
interesting twist. We've started looking forward to the game's
TV commercials more than the game. One year our former
company scored a win by having two commercials broadcast.

In the game of life, many people must compete daily to survive. Some fight from the day they're born, such as with physical
limitations, poverty, or other challenging situations. Each must
make specific choices if they're to survive and capture life's prizes, but relentless daily choices are often brutal. Revelation 4:10
says that when Jesus returns, we'll all lay down our trophies and
crowns before God. And they'll be worthless compared to the
crown and prize He'll give us.

■ ■ ■

*What are you competing for today? Kingdom crowns are the only
prizes that are worthwhile. Compete wisely.*

Day 3

LOVE-BOMB IMPERFECTION

This is how love is made complete among us so that
we will have confidence on the day of judgment: In this world
we are like Jesus. There is no fear in love. But perfect love
drives out fear, because fear has to do with punishment.
The one who fears is not made perfect in love.

1 JOHN 4:17–18

I want to get it right—*perfect. God must be punishing me.* I've
heard those words, sometimes laughingly, from the lips
of many people. But they're wrong. God doesn't punish; He
disciplines.

When Jesus—the only perfect man—walked the earth, He
didn't come just to instruct us; God loved us. And He demonstrated that love when He "love-bombed" our imperfect lives.
Jesus forever changed the definition of perfection. His perfect
love encompassed and penetrated the wound of sin, decimating
every fear in life, including the pressure to attain perfection.

A father disciplines a child for making wrong choices. He
loves the child and wants the child to mature in right ways.
If you feel God is punishing you, examine the choices you've
made. Were they made out of selfishness, jealousy, or fear? Face
God's discipline. Jesus' perfect love banishes all fear. Recognize
the fear of imperfection—and that it's keeping you from trusting God fully and ultimately being confident in His perfect love,
which completes us.

■ ■ ■

*What are you afraid of? Relinquish that hidden fear to Him today
and walk in the peace and confidence of His perfection.*

Day 4

MASTER OF MUSIC

You make me glad by your deeds, LORD;
I sing for joy at what your hands have done.

PSALMS 92:4

I asked my three-year-old daughter where her seven-year-old sister was, and she told me she was playing her *ee ee ee ee*—also known as her violin. She didn't know the official name for the instrument, just what it sounded like—and frankly, most of the time she was right!

The strings on a violin or other stringed instruments must be strung correctly and pulled to the right tension (tuned) for music to be played. The wrong tension can produce an awful noise rather than a sweet tone. A masterful ear is needed to hear the difference and adjust the tension accordingly.

Like strings on a musical instrument, the tensions of the world can influence our lives, keeping us tightly wound or too loose for use. God is the musical master of our lives. He wants to stretch us with His ultimate plan to produce His breathtakingly beautiful-sounding music. His tension and stretching is always right, and His goal is to create joy and the sound of hope. It's the music of God in our lives that will move others toward His heart. But, if we're not letting God be the Master of our internal music, we may sound like *ee ee ee ee*. So let God's healing music be heard.

■ ■ ■

What kind of music do people hear when they see you? Tune yourself up today to make beautiful music.

Journal

WEEK

48

Day 1

MYSTICAL JOURNEY

So we fix our eyes not on what is seen, but on what is unseen,
since what is seen is temporary, but what is unseen is eternal.

2 CORINTHIANS 4:18

*J*obs and lifestyles can consume our time like a ravenous beast. In Hollywood, it's not uncommon for industry professionals to work sixty-plus hours a week. Our culture keeps us competitive and never satisfied, driving us to consume more, learn more, and become a superstar in whatever we're pursuing. Our electronic devices, convenience foods, and smartphone apps, which are designed to give us more time, only allow us to fill the hours with more. We get caught up in what the world tells us we need to be or have to be happy.

Our striving for more comes from our soul's inner need for contentment, and we think more "stuff" will bring happiness. But what our soul really desires is the joy that comes only from a vibrant relationship with God. He made us and knows what we truly need to satisfy our deepest desires. The bottom line is, we'll never have enough in this broken world.

The Bible promises that God will bring an unnaturally peaceful life to us, and that's a mysterious thing to our culture. God wants us to realize that when we have Him we'll have enough, and that contentment is relative to our relationship with Him. It's a mystical journey that can only be learned when it's practiced.

■ ■ ■

What could you cut out of your schedule to allow for more time with God? Fix your eyes on the eternal.

Day 2

THE NAME

The name of the LORD is a fortified tower;
the righteous run to it and are safe.

PROVERBS 18:10

*N*ames given to children reflect the diversity and uniqueness of cultures and traditions, as well as their parents'
personalities. Most importantly, they're music to the ears of
those who cherish the child. God told Moses to call Him "I Am"
because He is, He was, and He is to come (Exodus 3:13–15).
God told Mary to call her son "Immanuel," meaning "God
with us," because God came down to be among us and with
us (Matthew 1:23). Jesus told us that God would send us "the
Advocate"—the Holy Spirit, our champion fighter and commu-
nicator on earth after Jesus ascended to heaven.

I believe there's an unseen world around us, one that has
ongoing spiritual warfare. Periodically throughout my life, I've
woken from a dream in terror. That terror, I believe, came from
the attacks of our enemy, satan, who roams this world seeking
whom He can devour (1 Peter 5:8).

I'm never sure why these dreams occur, but I've learned
how to survive and conquer them. My only escape has been
to call out the name of Jesus. The Bible instructs us to use His
name as our shield and our tower. He hears us "from the depths
of the pit" (Lamentations 3:55). You only need one name, Jesus.

■ ■ ■

*When was the last time you experienced terror? Next time, use your
defense shield—the name above all names, Jesus Christ—as your
defense.*

Day 3

THE RIGHT KIND OF SALT

> "You are the salt of the earth. But if the salt loses its saltiness,
> how can it be made salty again? It is no longer good for
> anything, except to be thrown out and trampled underfoot."
>
> MATTHEW 5:13

Salt is one of most essential elements of our existence. It's a preservative, an air purifier, a sleep inducer, a digestive aid—and it makes our food tastier. There are many varieties of salt in the world, but perhaps the healthiest is pink Himalayan salt. It contains over eighty-four minerals, so it does more than add zing to our food; it actually benefits our body. Pink Himalayan salt comes from salt mines located five thousand feet beneath the earth's surface in a region of Pakistan that has existed from the beginning of Earth's existence. It is said to be 99 percent pure due to the pressure of the earth on it over time. [38]

Jesus called us the "salt of the earth" for many reasons. He wanted us to recognize that humankind has been on the earth for a long time, and He's been at our side since the beginning. But He expects us to not be just any kind of salt. We're to be beneficial salt. We should add value to others' lives and be known by our distinctive flavor of influence.

If you aren't living a life *with* Christ, adding His permeating flavor wherever you go, you'll be useless and discarded.

∎ ∎ ∎

What can you do to bring healthy salt to others' lives? Think about your present usefulness and make changes if necessary.

Day 4

THE SCREAMING SILENCE

"I tell you," he replied, "if they keep quiet,
the stones will cry out."

LUKE 19:40

Martin Scorcese directed and cowrote the 2016 film *Silence*, based on the 1966 novel by Japanese novelist Shusaku Endo. The film is about seventeenth-century Jesuit priests who travel from Portugal to convert the Japanese to Christianity. Once the Japanese converts had heard God's voice, they couldn't deny Him. Their enemy—the Inquisitor—tried to destroy their physical symbols of faith, but he couldn't destroy what they heard inside.

One of the poignant conclusions I made after watching the film was how powerful the noise of God is in our inner souls. He can't be silenced, even though we may not be able to physically hear His voice. Our souls long for our Creator. Torture and death couldn't stop the spread of God's truth in Japan once they'd heard God's inner voice. They had to follow.

Still, we're afraid of the silence in our souls. One of the biggest ways satan is distracting us today is with noise. Many people need a sound device or TV playing to fall asleep. Our culture prefers earbuds with constantly streaming music, as well as video screens. Noise allows us to stay in denial of the questions of our soul and the voice of God. Silence means that God's voice will be heard, and it's just too terrifyingly confrontive. But God can't be silenced.

■ ■ ■

Confront the silence and listen to the voice of God. Then write down what He's saying to you and ask Him how to change.

Journal

WEEK

49

THE SON WILL COME OUT

The sun rises and the sun sets,
and hurries back to where it rises.

ECCLESIASTES 1:5

The Broadway musical *Annie* includes a show-stopping song, "Tomorrow," in which redhaired Little Orphan Annie sings about how, even though the day is gray, the sun is unrelenting—it will come out again. Solomon told us that too.

Sometimes we cause our own suffering and have to face the next day with its difficulties because of injuries we caused to others or even ourselves. As the saying says, "we have to face the music." Physical wounds have to be medicated and so do our heart wounds. Pain and suffering are inevitable. One of the most difficult days we can experience in life is the day after the death of a loved one. I know I felt that way when my mom died. Even though I had sung the praises of God all night and He had brought me peace, I still didn't want to face the next day and all the arrangements I'd have to make. But the sun came up.

Our great Creator only stopped the sun one time (Joshua 10:13) and it will keep coming out, regardless of the misery that awaits. He wants you to know that He will still be there tomorrow and the next day and all the days to come. God's Son is unrelenting to forgive and waiting to bring you peace. You can find comfort knowing He has "overcome the world" (John 16:33). Trust Him.

■ ■ ■

Are you dreading tomorrow? Grab ahold of God's Son-shine. What's one thing you can do right now to take a step toward Him?

FINAL CONSUMMATION

For it has been granted to you on behalf of Christ
not only to believe in him, but also to suffer for him,
since you are going through the same struggle you
saw I had, and now hear that I still have.

<small>PHILIPPIANS 1:29–30</small>

*W*riter and artist Flannery O'Connor wrote and prayed to God in her published personal journal, *A Prayer Journal*, that she wanted to be an artist. She said she understood that "it will be a life struggle with no consummation. When something is finished, it cannot be possessed. Nothing can be possessed but the struggle. All our lives are consumed in possessing struggle but only when the struggle is cherished and directed to a final consummation outside of this life is it of any value. … Dear God please help me be an artist, please let it lead to You."[39]

The life of Jesus was a struggle from His birth to His death. It was a life of suffering, but His eyes were not on His suffering and struggle but on the final goal—to please God the Father and fulfill the purpose for which God had placed Him on the earth. That purpose was to die for us and provide us a way back to heaven. When Jesus said, "It is finished" (John 19:30), as He hung on the cross, He had fulfilled His purpose. He gave His life over to a final consummation outside His own life—one that would lead all of us back to the Father.

■ ■ ■

What are you seeing as a final consummation? Be sure it leads back to God the Father.

■ ■

Day 3

THE THIRD WAY

Bless those who persecute you;
bless and do not curse.

ROMANS 12:14 NLT

*P*sychologists tells us that when we are persecuted, we will either fight or take flight. In Matthew 5:39, Jesus told us to "not resist an evil person" and "turn the other cheek." The Bible also says to "resist the devil" in James 4:7. Today's verse tells us to "bless those who persecute you." How can we take a stand and resist—fight and bless at the same time?

Walter Wink's book *Jesus and Non-Violence: A Third Way* teaches the way I believe God wants us to approach injustice and evil. It's a nonviolent way to take our stand the way Jesus did, with humbleness, wisdom, and forgiveness.

First, Christ wants us to recognize that we've all sinned (Romans 3:23) and all have evil within us. We're no better than the next person. Second, we're to actively pursue wisdom and knowledge so we know the truth that sets us free (John 8:32). Finally, when we act (and we *must* act and not cower or pursue violence), we are to do so with all manner of love and forgiveness because "love does not delight in evil but rejoices in truth" (1 Corinthians 13:6). "Standing our ground" in this manner "heaps burning coals" on our enemy's head and "overcomes evil with good" (Romans 12:20–21).

God hates evil (Proverbs 6:16–19). Let's bless our enemies with the third way.

■ ■ ■

When have you been treated unjustly? Study God's plan to take a righteous stand.

Day 4

THE WAITING GAME

Guide me in your truth and teach me, for you are
God my Savior, and my hope is in you all day long.

PSALMS 25:5

*O*ver the years, I've seen the heartbreak of talented individuals working in the media industry. For most, the struggle to find success and the waiting is always excruciating. One Christian woman who now works for a major movie studio went through ten interviews before she finally got hired. For her, the wait had a good ending, but her story isn't everyone's.

When I find myself in the waiting game, I've learned to pray—despite my circumstances or whatever frustrations I might feel—for what *God* would want for me. But waiting is never easy, so we often try to manipulate and push the boundaries of our agendas with schemes.

In the Bible, Sarah offered Abraham her maidservant, and Rachel had Jacob deceive Isaac, to help God along with their plans, rather than wait on Him. They thought they could assist Him, but it ended up complicating God's perfect plan and creating more suffering.

Thankfully, God always takes our mistakes and continues to move forward with His plan miraculously. So wait for him "all day long."

■ ■ ■

What are you waiting for that's not happening? Are you willing to wait for God's perfect plan? Drop whatever it is that you're scheming. Be patient. God doesn't need your help.

Journal

WEEK

50

Day 1

NEEDS, NOT WANTS

Come, all you who are thirsty, come to the waters;
and you who have no money, come, buy and eat! Come,
buy wine and milk without money and without cost.

ISAIAH 55:1

I drink water all day and night long. My aging body is drying and withering, so I have to stay hydrated. Without water we die.

In the Bible, God often associates Himself with water. He wants us to come to Him for living water (John 4:10) and for us to be His springs of living water (Zechariah 14:8–9). In the Scripture above, God also associates money with water. Without some kind of money, we also won't survive.

God said He'd supply all our needs, not our wants (Philippians 4:19). He said He'd give us enough for our journey, and He proved it to the children of Israel when Moses led them out of Egypt. They had to adjust to what they needed, not what they wanted, and it took forty years. They'd come from Egypt—the land of opulence and luxury—and had seen what they thought would bring them happiness and contentment. God had to teach them what would ultimately provide them with joy, abundance, and lasting satisfaction.

■ ■ ■

Do you want to drink from the Spring that never runs dry? What is God teaching you about money? Is your life going to testify to His provision and life, or will you continue to stress out with lifestyle choices that keep you from God's satisfying Spring?

Day 2

THORNS

Therefore, in order to keep me from becoming conceited, I was
given a thorn in my flesh, a messenger of Satan, to torment me.
Three times I pleaded with the Lord to take it away from me. But
he said to me, "My grace is sufficient for you, for my power is made
perfect in weakness." Therefore I will boast all the more gladly
about my weaknesses, so that Christ's power may rest on me.

2 CORINTHIANS 12:7–9

I have a hereditary hypothyroid condition, Hashimoto's
disease, that causes my body systems to lag. Every morning I take a pill to keep my body revving. This disease is my
thorn, and it reminds me daily of my humanity.

Paul revealed his humanity to us in Scripture, and how easy it
is to focus on our suffering, allowing it to rule our lives and draw
attention to us. When we allow our thorns to be our focus, we
are distracted off the path of God's purposes and blessings. We
all have thorns, and often we use social media to complain about
our injuries, illnesses, and bodily features we'd like to change.

Instead, let's use social media to demonstrate God's power
and blessings. Paul prayed to have his thorn taken away, but God
taught him a secret to surviving the difficulties of this world—
to embrace his imperfections, even brag about them, so others might see God's power and they, too, could overcome their
challenges. Paul embraced his imperfections and his humanity,
and when he did, people saw his authenticity and it was a powerful testimony.

■ ■ ■

*How can you change your attitude about a thorn you have in your
life? Write down one adjustment you can make. Live powerfully in
your weakness.*

304

Day 3

PERSPECTIVE

He has made everything beautiful in its time.
He has also set eternity in the human heart; yet no one
can fathom what God has done from beginning to end.

ECCLESIASTES 3:11

Camille Pissaro, one of the great French Impressionist painters, once said "it's a grave error to think that artists aren't closely tied to their time." In his time, the word *impressionist* was a term of criticism. But the artists turned it around, and it eventually became a definitive label and movement. Pissaro understood the power of art to influence culture and in using his art to change the perspective of the people.

On a recent trip to Bushwick, Brooklyn, I observed the artist community that's emerged there. Bushwick was originally built to be a warehouse community for New York City's industries—a treeless cement jungle of massive buildings and garage doors. Today it's full of passionate artists who have turned those bleak warehouse spaces and ugly industrial garage doors into places and works of art. They've created studios that have changed the landscape.

Great art comes from our soul and as Pissaro said, is a sign of the present time. This enclave of millennial art focuses on taking what's been discarded—vintage furniture, clothing, decorative bric-a-brac, and garage doors to create beauty and usefulness. God transforms our lives in the same way. He sees the discarded people of this world from a different perspective.

■ ■ ■

How is God speaking to you? Do something artistic and connect with His presence.

TONGUE LASHING REMEDY

> No one can tame the tongue;
> it is a restless evil and full of deadly poison.
>
> JAMES 3:8 NASB

When my mom was a child, my maternal grandmother favored her sons over her. Grandma would tell my mother that since she was a girl, she'd never amount to much and she wished she'd never been born. I wasn't very close to Grandma as a child (she didn't spend much time with me, maybe because I, too, was a girl), but I always loved her because my mother loved her through the forgiving eyes of Jesus. I came to understand as an adult that Grandma had circumstances in her life that had made her a bitter woman. Verbal abuse can't be unheard, and it's never forgotten. It can only be forgiven.

Satan uses our words to destroy hearts and minds with the ultimate goal of keeping us separated and bitter. In fact, the above Scripture says that "no one can tame the tongue." But God's not a "no one." He's a divine verbal surgeon who restores minds and hearts when poisonous verbal outbursts cut us to the core. But we have to purposefully replace the damage with restorative Scripture. The tongue can bring evil or it can bring God's restoration. Use your tongue and speak Scripture when the enemy uses words to destroy you.

■ ■ ■

How have God's healing words healed you? "By his wounds we are healed" (Isaiah 53:5).

Journal

WEEK

51

TRADITION

But the Pharisee was surprised when he noticed that Jesus
did not first wash before the meal. Then the Lord said to him,
"Now then, you Pharisees clean the outside of the cup
and dish, but inside you are full of greed and wickedness."

LUKE 11:38–39

"Tradition," the opening number in the 1964 Broadway musical *Fiddler on the Roof*, talks all about tradition in a Jewish
family and how the members (papas, mamas, sons, and daugh-
ters) are expected to do certain things in life because that's what
tradition dictates.

Tradition plays a part in Christians' lives as well. It often
influences the songs we sing, what our church services are like,
how we worship God, and the beliefs we hold.

Think about your own faith experience. Do you believe in
God because you were told to, having been raised to follow the
rules and traditions of your faith? Or have you experienced God
in your life personally and dedicated yourself to following Him
for that reason?

God doesn't get offended if you ask Him questions about
those hard life issues. He is there to answer them for you. He
says, "You will seek me and find me when you seek me with
all your heart." (Jeremiah 29:13). God looks at the heart, and
when you stand before Him on judgment day, following traditions won't help you.

■ ■ ■

*What traditions did you grow up with but have since left behind?
Determine to follow your heart and your own personal studied faith
of God and stop being a traditional Christian.*

EXPOSED

"You still lack one thing. Sell everything you have
and give to the poor, and you will have treasure in heaven.
Then come, follow me."

LUKE 18:22

*C*elebrity culture treasures perfection and beauty, valuing outward appearances and the accumulation of worldly treasures. In contrast, God looks at the heart.

Real life is messy, and it's not the picture of celebrity life. Being vulnerable and exposing our true selves is not what we want to post on social media. When we show our messes, we expose ourselves to public opinion and criticism, and in today's "look at me" culture, it's the last thing we want to do. But it's the one thing God asks us to do. We're to expose our need of Him and admit that we are like everyone else—vulnerable to the world's opinions. Why? Because it's about letting others see the struggle and how God brings us through it. We all have enough when we have the riches of God in our lives.

When you tell others about your struggles with finances, health issues, relationships, or abuse problems and how God was there at your side, you testify to His grace and provision. You become real and approachable. Pretenses crumble. It takes courage to let others see you naked and vulnerable, but it ultimately exposes truth and trust in God. So share your life and be a transparent believer.

■ ■ ■

How can you be a role model of transparency today? Expose your true self and let people see God's crystal-clear work being done in you.

Day 3

UNDYING ROOTS

So that Christ may dwell in your hearts through faith.
And I pray that you, being rooted and established in love,
may have power, together with all the Lord's holy people,
to grasp how wide and long and high and deep
is the love of Christ.

EPHESIANS 3:17—18

I stood in front of the simple display case in the small dusty museum room in the Mission of Charity in Kolkata, India, mesmerized by Mother Teresa's sandals. They were so tiny and had clearly been patched repeatedly. Viewing them brought the reality of her life into full view. She truly found her footing in God's undying love and joy.

It was peaceful inside the walls of the complex that continues to do her work, as well as in other global missions where the Sisters of Charity have given their lives. Their peaceful work is evident there, as well at their mission in Cairo, Egypt, in the middle of "Garbage City," where hundreds of Coptic Christians live and work. The Sisters of Charity have established a mission in the middle of the garbage piles to care for crippled and abandoned children and widows who have been discarded. When I visited that site, I saw tangible displays of God's hope and love there as well. The sisters' deep love for God is a powerful, awe-inspiring example of being rooted in His love.

■ ■ ■

Where are your undying roots of love growing? God is calling you to find your footing in His will.

UNFRIENDED

For all have sinned and fall short of the Glory of God.

ROMANS 3:23

Social media platforms were established to bring people together and create focused groups who "like" the same thing. Groups "follow" one another to gain a united voice and have been instrumental in starting movements and instigating uprisings. They've also created a lot of isolation. If you don't think the same as the group, you may be inclined to not speak out for fear of a massive "unfriending" that leaves you ostracized.

That's exactly what happened to Jesus. He made controversial statements that went against the beliefs of those in authority, challenging their interpretations of Scripture and the law. The religious leaders were devoted to God and thought they understood how to live godly lives, but their thinking was foggy and had become misguided by their own selfish desires, fears, pride, and stubbornness. So Jesus had to go to the outsiders to begin His ministry. He had to find people who were so broken they were willing to listen.

Established religions are groups. They're lead by well-meaning, devoted, good people, but they are human and aren't God. Jesus was and is the authority, and He teaches us to stay connected and never stop educating ourselves on His truth and defending it. This may mean that we will get "unfriended" from time to time. But we will keep our most important friend—Jesus.

■ ■ ■

When have you been "unfriended" in this way? Listen to God's voice and Word, and let Him deal with people's missteps. When you do give your opinion online, do it with grace.

Journal

WEEK

52

Day 1

UNLEASH YOUR GUILT—
YOU'RE FORGIVEN

Who is a God like you, who pardons sin and forgives the
transgression of the remnant of His inheritance? You do not
stay angry forever but delight to show mercy.

MICAH 7:18

One of the most horrific memories I have of raising my
kids is the time I got frustrated with my younger daughter while helping her practice her piano. She kept defiantly hitting the wrong key on the piano, so I bit her finger—to the horror of both of us. I didn't bite hard enough to break the skin, but I wanted it to sting. It was uncharacteristic of my parenting style, and I immediately asked her forgiveness as both of us cried. She forgave me (and we laugh about it now), but it was my loss of patience and maturity that I found unforgivable for a long time afterward.

Studies show that forgiving ourselves is one of the hardest things to do, especially when we've caused injury to someone else and even though we've been forgiven. So what can we do? Take a deep breath and accept our failings and God's forgiveness. One of the suggestions professional therapists give is to send ourselves an apology note. They have found that if we write the offense down, it helps us to release our emotional guilt and move on.

God delights in showing mercy, and His forgiveness is immediate. He *removes* our sins "as far as the east is from the west" (Psalm 103:12). So unleash your guilt and shame. You're forgiven.

■ ■ ■

*What's one thing you could write a note of apology to yourself for?
God has forgiven you, so isn't it about time you forgive yourself?*

Day 2

JUST LIKE JESUS

"No one has ever seen God, but the one and only Son,
who is himself God and is in closest relationship
with the Father, has made him known."

JOHN 1:18

My son-in-law, Chris, stood there laughing as he related to me how my three-year-old granddaughter had started saying a phrase he didn't even realize he used until he heard her repeat it. "I have to start paying more attention to what I'm saying," he said. "She picks up everything!"

"The apple doesn't fall far from the tree" is an adage used when observing how kids mimic or act like their parents. I often look at my husband and think, *He's just like his father.* There's just something in our DNA that makes us do and say things like our parents.

John was saying that in this Scripture verse. Just as I recognize similarities with my mother in myself, so do we with God and Jesus, who are one and the same. God also created us in His image (Genesis 1:27), and when we do things that mimic the Father, others see God in us. John went on to quote Jesus in John 14:7: "If you really know me, you will know my Father as well. From now on, you do know him and have seen him."

Do you really know Jesus? Have you developed a relationship with Him that's inseparable from Him?

■ ■ ■

How have you made God known by the choices you've made in life? Choose wisely so others will see Him and give Him glory.

Day 3

FINDING GOD
IN UNEXPECTED PLACES

"You will seek me and find me
when you seek me with all your heart."

JEREMIAH 29:13

Researchers tell us that the media listening and viewing habits of Christians and nonbelievers are virtually the same. Christian media is valuable, but we still have many improvements to make. As a media professional, I listen to and watch lots of mainstream media, and I've found that sometimes when I'm singing a secular tune, my heart and mind reverts to God and His love, not an earthly love (a common theme in most secular songs). I know the artists aren't singing about God, but my love for Him just seems to go there.

Having worked in Hollywood, I've been honored to get to know the Boone family. Debby Boone's hit song "You Light Up My Life" was on Billboard's top 100 song list for ten consecutive weeks in 1977, winning its songwriter, Joe Brooks, a Grammy for Song of the Year, an Academy Award for Best Song, a Golden Globe, and an ASCAP award. Debby will tell you that most people don't know that when she recorded the song, she wasn't singing to a love interest but to Jesus. She prayed that unsuspecting listeners would hear the song and feel God's love in their lives and not just an earthly romantic love.

When our hearts are seeking Him, we'll find Him in unexpected places.

■ ■ ■

What songs are you singing for God? Seek Him with all your heart and you'll find Him in the tunes you listen to every day.

AUTHORITATIVE DIRECTION

> Furthermore, just as they did not think it worthwhile to
> retain the knowledge of God, so God gave them over to a
> depraved mind, so that they do what ought not to be done.

ROMANS 1:28

Google Maps and Waze are smartphone apps that help us reach our destinations, but personally, I wonder if they're making me dumb. I've become so dependent on them it seems I can't find my way around Los Angeles anymore.

The church used to be a leading authority. We'd look to its leaders for wisdom not only on spiritual issues but on culture and politics. Now we rush to the Internet to find a date, learn how to live, or find out what's trending, never thinking of asking leaders in the church or even God, the Supreme Being. Have websites and social media become the new rulers—our modern-day gods of authority? Are we giving our minds over to them?

If we're to regain our authority as the body of Christ, we need to grow not only in our knowledge of God but in how media is manipulating our minds and choices. God wants us to be careful about where we're getting directions from in life. Don't let technology make you biblically and spiritually dumb.

■ ■ ■

Examine the sources that direct and influence your life. Remember, God is the number one authority.

ACKNOWLEDGMENTS

I'm first and foremost eternally grateful to my heavenly Father for His direction and redeeming grace. He's my constant mentor and the editor of my life.

My parents were influencers and directors of my life's path, but I would especially like to acknowledge my mother, who stood through many personal challenges. She was a constant force toward encouraging me in my faith in God. She's an example of why Jesus said to "train up a child in the way he should go. Even when he is old he will not depart from it" (Proverbs 22:6 NASB).

I'm also very grateful to Arnie Cole for his friendship and passion to encourage others to read the Bible. His influential work on why Bible reading is essential has impacted my life and became a direct influence on the writing of this book. Also, many thanks to Pamela Caudill, who, with Arnie, did the hard research and graciously provided updated information.

Many thanks to BroadStreet Publishing Group and their talented team who collaborated with me: Carlton Garborg, David Sluka, Bill Watkins, Christy Distler, and Kendall Moon. I'd especially like to thank Suzanne Niles for her consistent prayer and encouragement, who even now continues to champion me. She's blessed my life not only with inspiration but with sacrificial friendship.

Many thanks to my amazing kids, Bailey and Kelsey, my son-in-law, Chris, and my grandkids, Kennady and Clyde, who keep me grounded in love.

Finally, Phil Cooke, my husband, thank you, my love. Without your encouragement, my life would be vastly different. Your insights and expertise provide important guidance. I'm truly blessed to be married to the man of my dreams.

ABOUT THE AUTHOR

*K*athleen Cooke is a media executive, member of the Hollywood Screen Actors Guild, and a founding partner and the vice-president of Cooke Pictures, a media production company based in Burbank, California. She also cofounded the nonprofit organization The Influence Lab, where she leads and mentors Christian professionals in the entertainment industry.

She writes a weekly blog at kathleencooke.com and serves as founding editor of *InfluenceWomen*, a monthly digital journal. She has codirected two nationally recognized conferences, the Biola Media Conference and the ASCEND Women's Conference, and founded and directed the Hollywood chapter of Christian Women in Media. She is on the national boards of the Salvation Army, Hollywood Prayer Network, and 4Word Women.

With more than twenty-five years' experience in media and entertainment, she has a passion to see men and women discover their significance through a vibrant relationship with God and to flourish using their unique skills and talents to enrich God's kingdom.

Follow Kathleen on Twitter (@KathleenRCooke), Instagram (@KathleenRCooke), and Facebook (KathleenRCooke).

ABOUT THE AUTHOR

ABOUT THE AUTHOR

Kathleen Cooke is a media executive, member of the Hollywood Screen Actors Guild and a founding partner and the vice-president of Cooke Pictures, a media production company based in Burbank, California. She also cofounded the nonprofit organization The Influence Lab, where she leads and mentors Christian professionals in the entertainment industry.

She oversees daily blog at InfluenceWoman.com and serves as founding editor of Influence Woman, a monthly digital journal. She has produced two nationally recognized conferences, the Media Conference and the 2007 END Women's Conference, and founded and cofounded the Hollywood chapter of Christian Women in Media. She is on the editorial board of the Salvation Army's Holiness and Prayer Notebook, and a Word Woman.

With more than twenty-five years' experience in media and entertainment, she has a passion to see men and women discover their significance through a deliberate relationship with God and to flourish using their unique skills and talents to enrich God's kingdom.

Follow Kathleen on Twitter (@KathleenRCooke), Instagram (@KathleenRCooke), and Facebook (KathleenRCooke).

OTHER RESOURCES

The Center for Bible Engagement's full research and conclusions are available online, as well as the entire study: backtothebible.org/research.

ADDITIONAL RESOURCES

Ariely, Daniel. *Predictably Irrational*. New York: Harper Collins. 2008.

Brown, J. "SBC Leader Alarmed over Young Adults 'Dropping Out' of Churches." Agape Press, August 7, 2006. http://headlines.agape press.org/archive/8/72006e.asp (site discontinued).

Ovwigho, Pamela Caudill, Arnold Cole, and Alan Myatt. "Private Spiritual Practices: Bible Engagement and Moral Behavior." *Journal of Psychology and Christianity*, 35 (2016): 322–241.

"On the Verge of Walking Away? American Teens, Communication with God, and Temptations." Center for Bible Engagement, May 2009. http://backtothebible.org/files/web/docs/cbe/On_the _Verge_of_Walking_Away.pdfhttp://backtothebible.org/files /web/docs/cbe/On_the_Verge_of_Walking_Away.pdf.

NOTES

1 "Winning the Day Spiritually," Center for Bible Engagement, January 2009, http://www.backtothebible.org/files/web/docs/cbe/Temptation _Survey_Results.pdf, 7.

2 Arnold Cole and Pamela Caudill Ovwigho, "Understanding the Bible Engagement Challenge: Scientific Evidence for the Power of 4," Center for Bible Engagement, December 2009, http://www.backtothebible.org/ files/web/docs/cbe/Scientific_Evidence_for_the_Power_of_4.pdf, 1.

3 Ibid., 14.

4 Ibid., 6–7.

5 Ibid., 5.

6 Arnold Cole and Pamela Caudill Ovwigho, "Bible Engagement and Social Behavior: How Familiarity and Frequency of Contact with the Bible Affects One's Behavior," Center for Bible Engagement, December 2009, http://www.backtothebible.org/files/web/docs/cbe/Bible_Engagement _and_Social_Behavior.pdf, 5.

7 "What the Media Isn't Reporting on ISIS' Beheading of 21 Christian Men," *DalyFocus*, February 18, 2015, http://jimdaly.focusonthefamily .com/what-the-media-isnt-reporting-on-isis-beheading-of-21-christian -men/.

8 Cole and Ovwigho, "Bible Engagement," 4.

9 Ibid., 17.

10 For more information on the Young Creative Conference, see https:// www.facebook.com/YCLconference/.

11 Stephen R. Anderson, "How Many Languages Are There In the World?" *Linguistic Society of America*, https://www.linguisticsociety.org/content /how-many-languages-are-there-world.

12 www.urbandictionary.com

13 https://elev8.hellobeautiful.com/297815/opinionadd-no-more-porn- to-the-list-of-resolutions/

14 "Dietrich Bonhoeffer," *Geschichte: begreifen*, Gesellschaft zur Förderung von didaktischen Medien zur deutschen Geschichte, http://www.geschichte -begreifen.info/en/dietrich-bonhoeffer.html.

15 Adam Carter, "Heart, Stroke Patients Often Return to Unhealthy Life- styles," *CBC*, April 17, 2013, http://www.cbc.ca/news/canada/hamilton

/news/heart-stroke-patients-often-return-to-unhealthy-lifestyles-1.130 7707.

16 Matt de Neef, "Hidden Motors for Road Bikes Exist—Here's How They Work," *CyclingTips*, April 24, 2015, https://cyclingtips.com/2015/04 /hidden-motors-for-road-bikes-exist-heres-how-they-work/.

17 "Surrender Dorothy," *Wikipedia*, https://en.wikipedia.org/wiki /Surrender_Dorothy.

18 "Field of Dreams," *IMDb*, http://www.imdb.com/title/tt0097351/.

19 Monica Lewinsky, "The Price of Shame," *TED*, March 2015, https:// www.ted.com/talks/monica_lewinsky_the_price_of_shame#t-828681.

20 Paula Cocozza, "Serena Williams: Not Everyone's Going to Look the Way I Look," *The Guardian*, June 28, 2016, https://www.theguardian.com/ lifeandstyle/2016/jun/28/serena-williams-interview-beyonce-dancing -too-masculine-too-sexy (site discontinued).

21 "History," Crazy Water, http://drinkcrazywater.com/cw/crazy-water -history/.

22 Milagros Valdez, "The 10 Most Suicidal Cities in America," *Insider Monkey*, October 9, 2014, http://www.insidermonkey.com/blog/the-10-most -suicidal-cities-in-america-331367/6/.

23 "YouTube Yearly Costs for Storage/Networking—Estimate," *Suman Srinivasan's Code Blog*, April 14, 2012, https://sumanrs.wordpress.com /2012/04/14/youtube-yearly-costs-for-storagenetworking-estimate/.

24 Stephen J. Nichols, *The Reformation: How a Monk and a Mallet Changed the World* (Wheaton: Crossway, 2007), 91.

25 "Do Yourself a Favor … Forgive: An Interview with Joyce Meyer," *CBN*, http://www1.cbn.com/700club/do-yourself-favorforgive-interview -joyce-meyer.

26 "Garbage Dreams," *PBS/Independent Lens*, http://www.pbs.org /independentlens/garbage-dreams/film.html.

27 Ryan, "Garbage City and the Cave Church," *Reason to Believe*, July 11, 2007, http://reasontobelieve.blogspot.com/2007/07/garbage-city-and-cave -church.html.

28 Officialpsy, "Psy—Gangnam Style," *YouTube*, https://www.youtube. com/watch?v=9bZkp7q19f0.

29 David Green, *Giving It All Away … and Getting It All Back Again* (Grand Rapids: Zondervan, 2017), n.p.

30 Philip Connor and Jens Manuel Krogstad, "Key Facts about the World's Refugees," *Pew Research Center*, October 5, 2016, http://www.pewresearch .org/fact-tank/2016/10/05/key-facts-about-the-worlds-refugees/.

31 Ellen Francis and Lisa Barrington, "Aleppo Endgame Nears as Evacuation Resumes," *Reuters*, December 21, 2016, http://www.reuters.com/article /us-mideast-crisis-syria-idUSKBN14A1CL.

32 "Star Wars: Episode IV—A New Hope," *IMDb*, http://www.imdb.com /title/tt0076759/.

33 Consuming Fire Revival Channel, "Somewhere It's Snowing!" November 26, 2011, https://www.youtube.com/watch?v=HWriqKYi8x0.

34 William Shakespeare, *The Tragedy of Macbeth*, http://shakespeare.mit.edu /macbeth/full.html, act 5, scene 1.

35 Alexander Pope, "An Essay on Criticism," 1711.

36 John Kolbin, "How Much Do We Love TV? Let Us Count the Ways," *New York Times*, June 30, 2016, https://www.nytimes.com/2016/07/01 /business/media/nielsen-survey-media-viewing.html?_r=2.

37 Claudia Aguirre, "From Medication to Meditation: A Brief History of Depression Therapy," *Huffington Post/United Kingdom*, October 29, 2016, http://www.huffingtonpost.co.uk/dr-claudia-aguirre/depres-sion-brief-history_b_8372402.html. _<<The _ = an underscore.>>

38 "Top 6 Essential Health Benefits of Sea Salt," *Dr. Axe*, https://draxe. com/10-benefits-celtic-sea-salt-himalayan-salt/.

39 Flannery O'Connor, *A Prayer Journal* (New York: Farrer, Straus, and Giroux, 2013), April 14, 1947.

Journal

Journal

Journal

Journal

Journal

Journal

Journal

Journal

KathleenCooke.com